Contents

Introduction

This publication is the second report from the 2001 Census of Population for Northern Ireland, produced in accordance with the provisions of the Census Act (Northern Ireland) 1969. The first report, published in September 2002, provided population counts by age and sex. This report now provides summary statistics for the majority of Census questions and topics. They are mainly presented as percentages of population totals, facilitating comparisons between geographical areas. They are presented in this report for Northern Ireland, Local Government Districts, Health and Social Services Boards, Education and Library Boards, Parliamentary Constituencies and NUTS Level III (European Union Nomenclature of Units for Territorial Statistics) Areas. The tables will also be available electronically down to Electoral Ward and Census Output Area level on the NISRA website www.nisra.gov.uk. The tables presented in this report form only a small subset of the results from the 2001 Census, and information on further results is provided below.

As with all Census outputs, this report was made possible by the co-operation of members of the public in responding to the Census; the commitment of the Census field staff in delivering and collecting forms; and the assistance of many other people and organisations throughout all aspects of the Census. The Registrar General would like to thank all those who have contributed to this work.

Background to the 2001 Census

Legislation

The Census Act (Northern Ireland) 1969 allows for the carrying out of a Census no less than five years after the previous Census. However various other legislative requirements need to be fulfilled before a Census can be held. The first stage in this process was the publication of The White Paper 'The 2001 Census of Population' which set out the reasons for holding a Census, the proposed questions, operational methodology and format of results. The White Paper was produced in March 1999, two years before the Census, to ensure sufficient time for public discussion of proposals. Prior to every Census, a Census Order is required, which states the date of the Census, the people who are required to complete the form, those who are to be included on the form and the topics on which questions will be asked. The operational aspects of the Census also require legislative approval. This information was set out in the Census Regulations, which contained details of how the Census was to be conducted and included a copy of the Census form.

Fieldwork

The Census was designed to collect information on the resident population on Census Day - 29 April 2001. Ahead of this day enumerators delivered Census forms to every identified household space and communal establishment. Residents were asked to complete the forms with their information, as correct on Census Day, and to return the completed forms by post. Where Census Office did not receive a form through the post, the enumerator visited the address in order to collect the form by hand. Special arrangements were made to enumerate the Armed Forces and people sleeping rough.

Processing

Returned forms were fed through scanning machinery which captured all the ticked responses and stored written answers in digital form. The latter were coded into categories either by automatic systems which recognise terms given in response to questions, or by manual coding. These data then underwent an edit process to ensure that the data were consistent, and an imputation process to supply responses for questions which had not been completed on the original form.

Coverage of the population

The results in this report all relate to the usually resident population of Northern Ireland on Census Day, 29 April 2001. Students are recorded at their term-time address. In contrast to the 1991 Census, information on visitors has not been collected. The Census placed a legal obligation on every household in which someone was usually resident on Census Day, and on every person who was a usual resident of a communal establishment, to complete a Census form. As no Census of Population succeeds in collecting information from every resident, a methodology (The One Number Census) was developed to adjust the results to take account of any undercount and thus provide an accurate estimate of the total population and its characteristics. The One Number Census methodology was developed with the assistance of academic experts and was subject to consultation and peer review. The work involved matching the results of the Census enumeration with those of an independent large scale Census Coverage Survey of 10,000 households, conducted shortly after the Census. The response rate in the Census Coverage Survey was 92 per cent. This enabled the number and characteristics of those not enumerated in the Census to be estimated and this information was used to produce Census results, including those not enumerated in the original count. The figures presented here, as with all reports on the 2001 Census, have been adjusted to take account of under-enumeration. Administrative registers and demographic estimates were used to quality assure the final estimates. Further details on the methodology to adjust for under-enumeration can be found at www.nisra.gov.uk.

Comparability with 1991

The Census is designed to provide the most accurate possible picture of the population on the day the Census is taken. Comparisons of the results contained in this report with counts from the 1991 Census will be affected by changes in the Local Government District boundaries, changes in definitions, and adjustment for under-enumeration in the 2001 Census figures. Where comparisons between 1991 and 2001 Census results are required, the effects of the differences noted above can be mitigated by comparing differences between percentages calculated from the respective bases in each Census, rather than measuring the difference between the actual counts at each Census. Users interested in changes in population size are advised to use the mid-year population estimates, which are designed to measure such changes.

Information in this Report

This Report provides Census results for Northern Ireland and a range of local authority and administrative areas as constituted on Census Day, 29 April 2001. The results are based on the information collected from the Census forms. Copies of the Census forms will be contained in the forthcoming 2001 Census Definitions Volume. All questions included in the 1991 Census were included in the 2001 Census with the exception of questions relating to usual address and whereabouts on Census night, fertility and professional/vocational qualifications and household accommodation questions on water supply and domestic sewage disposal. The answer categories in some questions, such as educational qualifications, were updated, while questions on religion and economic activity have been restructured. There were also new questions on ethnic group, general health, the provision of unpaid care, time since last paid employment, the size of work force at place of work, supervision of employees, lowest floor level of accommodation and whether all rooms in a household were located on a single floor.

The Census questions asked of all people covered:
- relationship to others in the household
- sex, age (date of birth) and marital status
- whether schoolchild/student
- term-time address (where applicable)
- Irish language
- religion or religion brought up in

- country of birth
- ethnic group
- general health
- provision of unpaid care
- long term illness
- usual address one year ago

whilst questions for those aged 16 to 74 covered:
- educational qualifications
- economic activity and employment status
- number of employees at place of work
- occupation and industry of employment
- address of workplace
- means of travel to work
- hours worked

In addition, the person filling in the form in each household was asked about:
- type of accommodation and whether self-contained
- number of rooms
- availability of bath/shower and toilet
- lowest floor level and whether all rooms on one level
- presence of central heating
- availability of cars or vans
- tenure
- landlord

Finding Information in this Report

This Report contains 33 tables, covering all topics contained in the Census. Within each table, results are presented for Northern Ireland's 26 Local Government Districts. Statistics are also provided for Health and Social Services Boards, Education and Library Boards and NUTS level III (European Union Nomenclature of Units for Territorial Statistics) areas; each of these geographical areas are the exact aggregates of Local Government Districts. Finally, statistics are also provided for Northern Ireland's 18 Assembly and Parliamentary constituencies; these constituencies are exact aggregates of Electoral Wards.

The actual counts underlying the percentages in this report are available on the NISRA website.

Key Statistics for Northern Ireland's 582 Electoral Wards are available on the NISRA website at www.nisra.gov.uk. Similar statistics for Census Output Areas will be made available in 2003.

Census Definitions

Key Census definitions on persons, households and communal establishments are given below, and details on all 2001 Census definitions and classifications can be found in the metadata section of the Census web site www.nisra.gov.uk. This will include a Census glossary together with details on 2001 Census output classifications, differences between parts of the UK, comparability with the 1991 Census, Census concepts and definitions, data classifications, and standard derived variables. A printed Census Definitions volume will be available in February 2003.

Persons: Results from the 2001 Census of Population relate to the usually resident population; a usual resident is defined as someone who resides at that address most of the time. The usually resident population includes persons temporarily away on Census Day (for example on holiday, on business, in hospital or visiting family), persons who work away from home for part of the time, students at their term-time address, babies born before Census Day even if still in hospital, and persons staying at that address if they have no other usual address.

Households: A household comprises one person living alone, or a group of persons not necessarily related living at the same address with common housekeeping, that is, sharing either a living-room or sitting-room or at least one meal a day.

Communal establishments: A communal establishment is defined as an establishment providing managed residential accommodation, where managed means full-time or part-time supervision of the accommodation.

Fuller details of these terms and other Census definitions can be found on the NISRA website at www.nisra.gov.uk.

Quality of the results

The use of the One Number Census methodology means that the results of the 2001 Census cover the entire population of Northern Ireland and are the most reliable achievable. The results are nonetheless subject to potential errors from a variety of sources including incorrect information provided on forms, sampling error relating to estimates derived through the One Number Census process, and errors introduced during processing and imputation. Some elements of incorrect information have been corrected during an edit process and, following this, the results have undergone an extensive quality assurance process including checks against administrative sources.

Further information on accuracy, coverage and imputation rates is provided on the NISRA website. A detailed report on the quality of Census results will be published in 2003.

Confidentiality

The Registrar General has taken steps to ensure that the confidentiality of respondents is fully protected. All published results from the Census have been subject to statistical processes to ensure that individuals cannot be identified. One of these processes, small cell adjustment, may result in marginally different results between tables reporting the same statistic, however any differences between the figures will be very small. An example of this is seen in table KS06 of this report where the populations of some Local Government Districts differ slightly from other tables. A description of the small cell adjustment process is available on the NISRA website at www.nisra.gov.uk.

Further Information

Equivalent Key Statistics tables for Northern Ireland's 582 Electoral Wards are available on the NISRA website. Key Statistics for areas within Electoral Wards will be released early in 2003; for more information see the NISRA website.

Standard Tables and Census Area Statistics, which provide more detailed cross-tabular Census output, will follow these results. A timetable for the release of these results is included in the Census Output Prospectus which can be obtained on request from Census Customer Services or from the NISRA website at www.nisra.gov.uk.

All Census results are available in electronic format from the NISRA website at www.nisra.gov.uk.

Further information is available from the Northern Ireland Statistics and Research Agency website www.nisra.gov.uk and Census Customer Services:

Census Customer Services
McAuley House
2-14 Castle Street
Belfast, BT1 1SA

Telephone: +44 (0) 28 90348160
Fax: +44 (0) 28 90348161
E-mail: census.nisra@dfpni.gov.uk

Other Censuses in the UK

Separate Censuses were carried out, on the same day and using similar methodologies, in England and Wales and Scotland, under the authority of the respective Registrars General. Information on these Censuses is available from:

England and Wales
Census Customer Services
ONS
Titchfield
Fareham
Hants PO15 5RR

Telephone:+44 (0) 1329 813800
Fax:+44 (0) 1329 813587
Minicom: +44 (0) 1329 813669
E-mail: census.customerservices@ons.gov.uk

Scotland
General Register Office for Scotland
Census Division
Ladywell House
Ladywell Road
Edinburgh, EH12 7TF

Telephone: +44 (0) 131 314 4254
E-mail:customer@gro-scotland.gov.uk

Copyright and reproduction of material from this report

This report (excluding agency logos) may be reproduced free of charge in any format or medium for research, private study or for internal circulation within an organisation. This is subject to it being reproduced accurately and not used in a misleading context. The material must be acknowledged as Crown Copyright and the title of the report specified. This report can also be accessed at the Northern Ireland Statistics and Research Agency website www.nisra.gov.uk. For any other use of this material please apply for a Click-Use Licence on the HMSO website at http://www.hmso.gov.uk/click-use-home.htm, or by writing to HMSO at

The Licensing Division
St Clements House
2-16 Colegate
Norwich, NR3 1BQ

Fax: +44 (0)1603 723000
e-mail: hmsolicensing@cabinet-office.x.gsi.gov.uk

Key Statistics Tables

Table KS01: Usually Resident Population

Area	All persons	Percentage of persons who are:		Percentage of persons:		Area (hectares)[1]	Population density (number of persons per hectare)
		Male	Female	Living in households	Living in communal establishments		
Northern Ireland	**1,685,267**	**48.74**	**51.26**	**98.43**	**1.57**	**1,413,540**	**1.19**
Local Government District							
Antrim	**48,366**	50.12	49.88	96.32	3.68	57,686	0.84
Ards	**73,244**	48.82	51.18	99.12	0.88	37,619	1.95
Armagh	**54,263**	49.62	50.38	98.23	1.77	67,060	0.81
Ballymena	**58,610**	48.75	51.25	98.85	1.15	63,202	0.93
Ballymoney	**26,894**	49.54	50.46	99.27	0.73	41,820	0.64
Banbridge	**41,392**	50.02	49.98	99.29	0.71	45,263	0.91
Belfast	**277,391**	46.79	53.21	97.92	2.08	11,488	24.15
Carrickfergus	**37,659**	48.43	51.57	98.91	1.09	8,184	4.60
Castlereagh	**66,488**	47.63	52.37	98.69	1.31	8,514	7.81
Coleraine	**56,315**	47.73	52.27	98.11	1.89	48,551	1.16
Cookstown	**32,581**	49.69	50.31	99.09	0.91	62,244	0.52
Craigavon	**80,671**	49.28	50.72	99.31	0.69	37,842	2.13
Derry	**105,066**	48.67	51.33	98.29	1.71	38,731	2.71
Down	**63,828**	49.54	50.46	97.96	2.04	64,670	0.99
Dungannon	**47,735**	49.49	50.51	99.03	0.97	78,360	0.61
Fermanagh	**57,527**	50.09	49.91	98.85	1.15	187,582	0.31
Larne	**30,832**	49.06	50.94	99.24	0.76	33,567	0.92
Limavady	**32,422**	50.88	49.12	97.57	2.43	58,558	0.55
Lisburn	**108,694**	48.74	51.26	98.09	1.91	44,684	2.43
Magherafelt	**39,780**	50.38	49.62	99.50	0.50	57,280	0.69
Moyle	**15,933**	49.15	50.85	99.02	0.98	47,976	0.33
Newry and Mourne	**87,058**	49.50	50.50	99.11	0.89	90,243	0.96
Newtownabbey	**79,995**	48.33	51.67	98.32	1.68	15,056	5.31
North Down	**76,323**	48.24	51.76	97.52	2.48	8,149	9.37
Omagh	**47,952**	50.13	49.87	97.74	2.26	113,045	0.42
Strabane	**38,248**	50.02	49.98	99.56	0.44	86,165	0.44
Health and Social Services Board							
Eastern	**665,968**	47.84	52.16	98.12	1.88	175,124	3.80
Northern	**426,965**	48.97	51.03	98.51	1.49	435,567	0.98
Southern	**311,119**	49.53	50.47	99.02	0.98	318,768	0.98
Western	**281,215**	49.65	50.35	98.40	1.60	484,080	0.58

© Crown copyright 2002

Area	All persons	Percentage of persons who are:		Percentage of persons:		Area (hectares)[1]	Population density (number of persons per hectare)
		Male	Female	Living in households	Living in communal establishments		
Education and Library Board							
Belfast	277,391	46.79	53.21	97.92	2.08	11,488	24.15
North Eastern	394,384	48.91	51.09	98.46	1.54	373,324	1.06
South Eastern	388,577	48.60	51.40	98.25	1.75	163,636	2.37
Southern	343,700	49.55	50.45	99.03	0.97	381,012	0.90
Western	281,215	49.65	50.35	98.40	1.60	484,080	0.58
Parliamentary Constituency							
Belfast East	79,261	46.90	53.10	98.75	1.25	3,566	22.23
Belfast North	86,066	46.70	53.30	98.90	1.10	3,981	21.62
Belfast South	94,994	46.68	53.32	95.79	4.21	3,451	27.53
Belfast West	87,610	47.11	52.89	99.20	0.80	4,130	21.22
East Antrim	84,062	48.67	51.33	98.28	1.72	42,609	1.97
East Londonderry	88,737	48.88	51.12	97.91	2.09	107,109	0.83
Fermanagh and South Tyrone	91,127	49.85	50.15	98.85	1.15	250,602	0.36
Foyle	105,066	48.67	51.33	98.29	1.71	38,731	2.71
Lagan Valley	101,696	49.05	50.95	97.93	2.07	55,077	1.85
Mid Ulster	86,496	50.00	50.00	99.34	0.66	134,864	0.64
Newry and Armagh	100,950	49.42	50.58	98.60	1.40	108,152	0.93
North Antrim	101,437	49.02	50.98	98.99	1.01	152,998	0.66
North Down	85,992	48.20	51.80	97.53	2.47	11,388	7.55
South Antrim	99,810	49.43	50.57	97.91	2.09	71,314	1.40
South Down	104,658	49.78	50.22	98.50	1.50	129,801	0.81
Strangford	98,158	48.87	51.13	99.19	0.81	48,588	2.02
Upper Bann	102,947	49.41	50.59	99.29	0.71	47,969	2.15
West Tyrone	86,200	50.08	49.92	98.55	1.45	199,209	0.43
NUTS Level III							
Belfast	277,391	46.79	53.21	97.92	2.08	11,488	24.15
Outer Belfast	369,159	48.32	51.68	98.21	1.79	84,588	4.36
East of Northern Ireland	396,943	49.32	50.68	98.62	1.38	339,850	1.17
North of Northern Ireland	274,878	49.04	50.96	98.48	1.52	321,801	0.85
West and South of Northern Ireland	366,896	49.80	50.20	98.79	1.21	655,813	0.56

Note:
1 Area is on Census day, 29 April 2001.

KS01

9

Table KS02: Age[1] Structure

Area	All persons	Percentage of persons aged:																Mean age[2] of population in the area	Median age[2] of population in the area
		0-4	5-7	8-9	10-14	15	16-17	18-19	20-24	25-29	30-44	45-59	60-64	65-74	75-84	85-89	90 and over		
Northern Ireland	**1,685,267**	**6.84**	**4.29**	**3.01**	**7.87**	**1.61**	**3.17**	**2.89**	**6.49**	**6.81**	**22.22**	**17.19**	**4.37**	**7.31**	**4.56**	**0.96**	**0.43**	**35.83**	**34**
Local Government District																			
Antrim	48,366	7.39	4.60	2.96	7.52	1.47	2.81	2.68	6.41	7.68	23.92	17.78	4.20	6.02	3.47	0.73	0.36	34.63	33
Ards	73,244	6.34	3.84	2.70	6.99	1.41	2.80	2.42	5.56	6.30	22.81	20.08	4.69	7.52	4.96	1.06	0.50	37.76	37
Armagh	54,263	7.32	4.51	3.15	8.38	1.71	3.56	2.78	6.36	6.93	21.59	17.16	4.30	6.89	4.19	0.83	0.34	34.95	33
Ballymena	58,610	6.36	3.98	2.79	7.35	1.49	3.00	2.52	5.75	6.42	22.04	18.96	4.89	7.99	4.92	1.05	0.48	37.33	36
Ballymoney	26,894	7.17	4.15	2.85	7.99	1.52	3.22	2.60	5.79	7.00	22.43	17.25	4.52	7.43	4.90	0.81	0.37	36.05	34
Banbridge	41,392	7.19	4.38	2.86	7.64	1.55	2.99	2.69	5.79	6.96	23.87	17.27	4.24	6.92	4.30	0.95	0.38	35.65	34
Belfast	277,391	5.99	3.86	2.89	7.42	1.56	2.99	3.61	8.39	7.26	20.85	15.52	4.38	8.20	5.34	1.18	0.55	36.55	34
Carrickfergus	37,659	6.47	4.24	2.89	7.41	1.62	2.77	2.55	5.84	6.37	24.30	17.83	4.45	7.46	4.52	0.83	0.45	36.52	36
Castlereagh	66,488	6.57	4.08	2.96	6.89	1.25	2.34	2.05	4.62	5.94	24.89	17.25	4.72	9.12	5.81	1.03	0.48	38.33	37
Coleraine	56,315	6.71	4.01	2.72	7.40	1.51	2.86	3.00	7.08	6.12	21.77	17.66	5.02	7.69	4.97	1.07	0.42	36.83	35
Cookstown	32,581	7.25	4.65	3.24	8.94	1.86	3.77	2.82	6.78	7.17	21.24	16.72	4.06	6.25	4.09	0.82	0.34	34.23	32
Craigavon	80,671	7.10	4.56	3.22	8.19	1.63	3.24	2.53	5.79	6.59	22.99	17.08	4.44	7.13	4.27	0.87	0.36	35.43	34
Derry	105,066	7.67	4.80	3.36	9.17	1.85	3.79	3.29	7.29	7.18	22.35	15.66	3.80	5.80	3.12	0.62	0.26	32.75	31
Down	63,828	6.93	4.61	3.28	8.32	1.71	3.38	2.99	6.08	6.21	22.01	17.47	4.33	6.85	4.36	0.96	0.50	35.38	34
Dungannon	47,735	7.51	4.56	3.30	8.67	1.76	3.58	2.80	6.28	7.24	21.13	16.49	4.20	7.07	4.25	0.81	0.36	34.63	32
Fermanagh	57,527	6.83	4.27	2.82	8.32	1.85	3.66	2.75	5.68	6.52	21.15	18.05	4.26	7.29	4.99	1.11	0.45	36.18	35
Larne	30,832	6.19	3.91	2.92	7.31	1.48	2.93	2.35	4.97	5.98	23.34	18.84	5.00	8.23	5.06	1.02	0.48	37.88	37
Limavady	32,422	7.59	4.71	3.25	8.28	1.71	3.28	3.16	6.95	8.22	22.67	16.56	3.87	5.50	3.33	0.66	0.26	33.32	31
Lisburn	108,694	7.18	4.63	3.25	7.92	1.54	3.16	2.73	5.99	6.50	23.58	17.42	4.20	6.76	3.91	0.81	0.39	35.11	34
Magherafelt	39,780	7.64	4.80	3.18	8.67	1.77	3.41	2.78	6.88	7.85	21.85	15.93	3.79	6.45	3.91	0.81	0.29	33.83	31
Moyle	15,933	6.96	3.87	2.89	8.13	1.85	3.38	2.71	5.34	6.30	20.45	18.55	5.09	7.68	5.20	1.15	0.45	36.96	36
Newry and Mourne	87,058	7.76	4.81	3.32	8.93	1.76	3.56	2.95	6.45	6.63	21.87	16.24	4.03	6.69	3.92	0.78	0.31	34.02	32
Newtownabbey	79,995	6.38	4.03	2.82	7.04	1.42	2.75	2.75	6.21	6.79	22.91	18.01	4.77	8.19	4.61	0.90	0.41	37.04	36
North Down	76,323	5.59	3.58	2.52	6.74	1.42	2.89	2.55	5.56	5.97	21.61	20.52	4.62	8.18	6.06	1.49	0.68	39.26	39
Omagh	47,952	7.54	4.89	3.08	8.51	1.84	3.77	2.95	6.64	7.19	21.59	16.57	3.89	6.31	3.97	0.92	0.34	34.09	32
Strabane	38,248	7.99	4.51	3.08	8.62	1.84	3.47	2.92	6.09	7.48	21.62	16.49	4.30	6.78	3.77	0.75	0.30	34.22	32
Health and Social Services Board																			
Eastern	665,968	6.33	4.05	2.93	7.41	1.51	2.96	3.00	6.76	6.65	22.11	17.26	4.44	7.85	5.10	1.11	0.52	36.83	35
Northern	426,965	6.79	4.21	2.90	7.63	1.56	3.01	2.69	6.21	6.78	22.56	17.79	4.59	7.41	4.53	0.92	0.41	36.23	35
Southern	311,119	7.40	4.60	3.20	8.43	1.69	3.41	2.75	6.15	6.81	22.26	16.79	4.24	6.93	4.16	0.84	0.35	34.86	33
Western	281,215	7.51	4.66	3.15	8.71	1.83	3.66	3.06	6.65	7.21	21.91	16.52	3.98	6.29	3.76	0.79	0.32	33.55	32

KS0.2

Area	All persons	Percentage of persons aged:																Mean age² of population in the area	Median age² of population in the area
		0-4	5-7	8-9	10-14	15	16-17	18-19	20-24	25-29	30-44	45-59	60-64	65-74	75-84	85-89	90 and over		
Education and Library Board																			
Belfast	277,391	5.99	3.86	2.89	7.42	1.56	2.99	3.61	8.39	7.26	20.85	15.52	4.38	8.20	5.34	1.18	0.55	36.56	34
North Eastern	394,384	6.75	4.18	2.87	7.53	1.53	2.95	2.68	6.16	6.75	22.67	17.88	4.64	7.51	4.57	0.92	0.41	36.39	35
South Eastern	388,577	6.57	4.18	2.96	7.40	1.47	2.94	2.56	5.61	6.21	23.02	18.51	4.49	7.60	4.93	1.05	0.50	37.02	36
Southern	343,700	7.38	4.60	3.20	8.48	1.70	3.44	2.76	6.21	6.84	22.17	16.78	4.22	6.86	4.15	0.84	0.35	34.80	33
Western	281,215	7.51	4.66	3.15	8.71	1.83	3.66	3.06	6.65	7.21	21.91	16.52	3.98	6.29	3.76	0.79	0.32	33.95	32
Parliamentary Constituency																			
Belfast East	79,261	5.69	3.64	2.64	6.65	1.32	2.53	2.18	5.00	6.40	22.52	17.33	4.89	9.75	7.16	1.54	0.73	39.98	39
Belfast North	86,066	6.36	4.24	3.10	7.98	1.63	3.19	2.92	6.04	6.22	20.36	16.18	4.82	9.41	5.80	1.19	0.56	37.50	36
Belfast South	94,994	5.23	3.18	2.28	5.62	1.17	2.12	4.67	12.69	9.28	21.24	14.65	3.73	7.32	5.03	1.22	0.58	36.15	32
Belfast West	87,610	7.42	4.90	3.84	9.93	2.11	4.15	3.61	7.09	5.87	20.73	14.67	4.04	6.97	3.76	0.63	0.27	33.10	30
East Antrim	84,062	6.42	4.10	2.87	7.33	1.52	2.78	2.80	5.68	6.35	23.89	18.02	4.59	7.74	4.58	0.90	0.43	36.81	36
East Londonderry	88,737	7.03	4.26	2.91	7.72	1.59	3.01	3.06	7.03	6.89	22.10	17.26	4.60	6.89	4.37	0.92	0.36	35.55	34
Fermanagh and South Tyrone	91,127	6.94	4.31	2.95	8.35	1.79	3.60	2.71	5.79	6.75	21.23	17.55	4.35	7.40	4.83	1.02	0.43	35.94	34
Foyle	105,066	7.67	4.80	3.36	9.17	1.85	3.79	3.29	7.29	7.18	22.35	15.66	3.80	5.80	3.12	0.62	0.26	32.76	31
Lagan Valley	101,696	6.92	4.31	2.95	7.13	1.37	2.77	2.42	5.50	6.77	24.38	17.85	4.53	7.34	4.38	0.93	0.45	36.43	35
Mid Ulster	86,496	7.62	4.78	3.28	8.88	1.84	3.60	2.85	6.86	7.53	21.41	16.24	3.84	6.27	3.91	0.79	0.31	33.75	31
Newry and Armagh	100,950	7.50	4.64	3.21	8.57	1.72	3.58	2.88	6.56	6.84	21.59	16.71	4.16	6.85	4.07	0.79	0.32	34.52	33
North Antrim	101,437	6.67	4.01	2.82	7.65	1.56	3.12	2.57	5.70	6.56	21.89	18.44	4.82	7.79	4.96	1.00	0.44	36.97	36
North Down	85,992	5.53	3.56	2.53	6.76	1.40	2.88	2.50	5.43	5.89	21.47	20.55	4.72	8.30	6.25	1.53	0.71	39.52	39
South Antrim	99,810	6.95	4.37	2.94	7.32	1.48	2.84	2.52	6.18	7.18	23.68	18.37	4.51	6.75	3.75	0.78	0.37	35.65	34
South Down	104,658	7.27	4.64	3.28	8.66	1.74	3.43	2.99	6.23	6.38	21.81	17.04	4.17	6.80	4.23	0.90	0.41	34.84	33
Strangford	98,158	6.63	4.07	2.87	7.12	1.39	2.77	2.43	5.36	6.23	23.88	19.20	4.66	7.45	4.57	0.93	0.46	37.12	36
Upper Bann	102,947	7.11	4.54	3.16	8.11	1.62	3.22	2.56	5.78	6.68	23.28	17.06	4.42	7.02	4.21	0.87	0.35	35.38	34
West Tyrone	86,200	7.74	4.72	3.08	8.56	1.84	3.64	2.94	6.39	7.32	21.61	16.53	4.07	6.52	3.88	0.84	0.32	34.15	32
NUTS Level III																			
Belfast	277,391	5.99	3.86	2.89	7.42	1.56	2.99	3.61	8.39	7.26	20.85	15.52	4.38	8.20	5.34	1.18	0.55	36.56	34
Outer Belfast	369,159	6.50	4.14	2.92	7.25	1.44	2.83	2.56	5.69	6.34	23.34	18.20	4.53	7.86	4.91	1.01	0.48	37.11	36
East of Northern Ireland	396,943	6.80	4.29	2.98	7.66	1.54	3.04	2.60	5.80	6.57	22.89	18.22	4.53	7.21	4.47	0.95	0.44	36.26	35
North of Northern Ireland	274,878	7.42	4.47	3.10	8.45	1.73	3.41	3.06	6.78	7.06	22.07	16.61	4.27	6.56	3.91	0.79	0.32	34.43	32
West and South of Northern Ireland	366,896	7.43	4.64	3.16	8.64	1.79	3.61	2.84	6.40	6.99	21.53	16.74	4.09	6.75	4.19	0.87	0.35	34.58	33

Notes:
1 'Age' is age at last birthday.
2 'Mean age' and 'Median age' are calculated using age in years at last birthday. To estimate 'Mean age' including part-years add 0.50 to the value shown in the table.

Table KS03: Living Arrangements[1]

Area	All persons aged 16 and over in households	Living in a couple			Not living in a couple			
		Married or re-married	Cohabiting	Single (never married)	Married or re-married[2]	Separated (but still legally married)	Divorced	Widowed
				Percentage of persons aged 16 and over in households:				
Northern Ireland	**1,261,257**	**51.47**	**4.26**	**29.67**	**0.56**	**3.34**	**3.40**	**7.30**
Local Government District								
Antrim	**35,016**	55.83	4.89	26.07	0.51	3.07	3.56	6.07
Ards	**57,019**	57.07	5.19	23.55	0.41	2.68	3.81	7.29
Armagh	**39,745**	54.96	2.53	29.92	0.65	2.67	2.20	7.08
Ballymena	**45,059**	55.63	4.11	26.61	0.39	2.91	3.44	6.91
Ballymoney	**20,329**	54.61	3.90	28.37	0.46	2.73	2.83	7.10
Banbridge	**31,319**	56.62	4.06	26.47	0.48	2.54	2.95	6.88
Belfast	**211,573**	39.50	5.19	36.65	0.67	4.89	4.27	8.84
Carrickfergus	**28,730**	55.84	6.06	23.27	0.39	3.32	4.05	7.07
Castlereagh	**51,159**	56.97	4.43	23.91	0.41	2.72	3.58	7.98
Coleraine	**42,686**	52.37	4.79	28.33	0.49	2.87	3.95	7.19
Cookstown	**23,830**	53.97	2.55	31.33	0.59	2.59	2.26	6.70
Craigavon	**60,200**	53.33	4.27	27.37	0.55	3.42	3.76	7.30
Derry	**75,090**	46.89	3.93	34.37	0.62	4.71	3.65	5.82
Down	**46,676**	53.85	4.10	29.03	0.54	2.82	2.87	6.79
Dungannon	**34,976**	53.12	2.34	31.84	0.70	2.51	2.22	7.25
Fermanagh	**43,001**	52.02	3.14	32.18	0.58	2.42	2.08	7.57
Larne	**23,882**	54.20	5.46	25.06	0.52	2.99	3.71	8.06
Limavady	**23,350**	53.97	4.22	30.18	0.58	2.35	2.92	5.78
Lisburn	**79,973**	54.48	4.77	26.53	0.50	3.44	3.73	6.55
Magherafelt	**29,217**	53.09	2.74	32.83	0.52	2.42	1.91	6.48
Moyle	**12,001**	51.03	2.90	31.63	0.74	3.11	2.81	7.78
Newry and Mourne	**63,185**	52.65	2.55	31.74	0.66	3.04	2.59	6.76
Newtownabbey	**61,307**	55.77	5.15	24.54	0.41	3.11	3.74	7.28
North Down	**59,320**	56.47	5.22	22.78	0.55	2.69	4.29	8.00
Omagh	**34,487**	52.21	2.50	32.88	0.61	2.71	2.24	6.84
Strabane	**28,127**	50.85	3.11	33.08	0.66	3.30	2.26	6.75
Health and Social Services Board								
Eastern	**505,720**	48.93	4.95	29.95	0.56	3.74	3.94	7.93
Northern	**322,057**	54.57	4.46	27.18	0.47	2.93	3.36	7.02
Southern	**229,425**	53.84	3.17	29.58	0.61	2.93	2.82	7.05
Western	**204,055**	50.23	3.44	33.00	0.61	3.42	2.81	6.49

KS03

Area	All persons aged 16 and over in households	Living in a couple		Not living in a couple				
		Married or re-married	Cohabiting	Single (never married)	Married or re-married[2]	Separated (but still legally married)	Divorced	Widowed
Education and Library Board								
Belfast	211,573	39.50	5.19	36.65	0.67	4.89	4.27	8.84
North Eastern	298,227	54.62	4.61	26.85	0.47	2.96	3.45	7.04
South Eastern	294,147	55.71	4.78	25.14	0.48	2.92	3.70	7.27
Southern	253,255	53.86	3.11	29.74	0.61	2.90	2.77	7.01
Western	204,055	50.23	3.44	33.00	0.61	3.42	2.81	6.49
Parliamentary Constituency								
Belfast East	62,506	48.90	5.05	27.09	0.57	3.64	4.74	10.01
Belfast North	65,087	40.70	4.90	32.81	0.64	5.67	5.07	10.21
Belfast South	74,514	38.48	5.97	41.64	0.64	2.77	3.46	7.04
Belfast West	62,202	38.13	4.11	37.74	0.68	7.36	4.12	7.87
East Antrim	63,934	55.80	5.77	23.81	0.43	3.13	3.79	7.27
East Londonderry	66,036	52.94	4.59	28.99	0.53	2.69	3.58	6.69
Fermanagh and South Tyrone	67,933	52.56	2.87	31.79	0.63	2.41	2.19	7.55
Foyle	75,090	46.89	3.93	34.37	0.62	4.71	3.65	5.82
Lagan Valley	76,532	57.50	4.79	24.27	0.48	2.61	3.48	6.86
Mid Ulster	63,091	53.28	2.58	32.40	0.57	2.54	2.04	6.58
Newry and Armagh	73,695	52.39	2.61	31.45	0.67	3.15	2.56	7.17
North Antrim	77,389	54.65	3.86	27.85	0.46	2.90	3.18	7.10
North Down	66,902	56.39	5.21	22.65	0.54	2.72	4.34	8.16
South Antrim	74,711	57.22	4.88	24.92	0.46	2.90	3.30	6.33
South Down	76,347	54.71	3.24	29.87	0.59	2.57	2.43	6.60
Strangford	75,705	57.74	5.03	23.65	0.40	2.63	3.59	6.96
Upper Bann	76,969	53.83	4.35	27.05	0.53	3.31	3.73	7.20
West Tyrone	62,614	51.60	2.77	32.97	0.63	2.97	2.25	6.80
NUTS Level III								
Belfast	211,573	39.50	5.19	36.65	0.67	4.89	4.27	8.84
Outer Belfast	280,489	55.78	5.02	24.49	0.46	3.07	3.86	7.33
East of Northern Ireland	299,171	55.18	4.54	26.36	0.48	2.94	3.47	7.03
North of Northern Ireland	201,583	50.45	3.97	31.66	0.59	3.55	3.30	6.48
West and South of Northern Ireland	268,441	53.06	2.63	31.78	0.62	2.67	2.26	6.98

Percentage of persons aged 16 and over in households:

Notes:

1 The living arrangements variable is different to marital status. It combines information from both marital status and the relationship matrix. Therefore a person living as part of a 'cohabiting couple' could in fact be married (to someone else) but will not appear as married or separated in this classification.

2 A person not living in a couple can be classified married (or re-married) if they denote their marital status as married (or re-married) but have no spouse or partner resident in the household.

Table KS04: Marital Status

Area	All persons aged 16 and over	Percentage of persons aged 16 and over:					
		Single (never married)	Married	Re-married	Separated (but still legally married)	Divorced	Widowed
Northern Ireland	**1,287,211**	**33.11**	**48.45**	**2.67**	**3.84**	**4.12**	**7.81**
Local Government District							
Antrim	36,785	31.42	50.03	3.76	3.73	4.60	6.46
Ards	57,651	26.73	52.44	4.59	3.26	5.02	7.97
Armagh	40,661	32.31	52.80	1.77	2.98	2.64	7.50
Ballymena	45,726	29.34	52.31	2.98	3.48	4.15	7.73
Ballymoney	20,524	30.76	52.05	2.64	3.25	3.56	7.74
Banbridge	31,612	29.27	53.82	2.89	3.01	3.61	7.40
Belfast	217,130	41.28	36.94	2.18	5.46	4.86	9.28
Carrickfergus	29,140	27.23	50.78	4.80	4.00	5.28	7.90
Castlereagh	52,027	27.04	53.05	3.65	3.20	4.40	8.66
Coleraine	43,732	32.20	48.68	3.19	3.31	4.84	7.77
Cookstown	24,126	33.18	52.80	1.19	2.98	2.70	7.15
Craigavon	60,747	30.28	50.74	2.78	3.93	4.52	7.75
Derry	76,861	37.87	44.80	1.61	5.32	4.17	6.23
Down	47,963	32.44	50.76	2.45	3.26	3.53	7.56
Dungannon	35,420	33.75	51.92	1.38	2.76	2.60	7.58
Fermanagh	43,663	34.67	50.34	1.58	2.82	2.52	8.07
Larne	24,109	28.70	50.51	3.78	3.63	4.84	8.54
Limavady	24,138	34.16	50.94	2.13	2.93	3.78	6.06
Lisburn	82,040	30.45	50.40	3.39	4.07	4.66	7.03
Magherafelt	29,416	34.89	52.13	1.23	2.79	2.25	6.70
Moyle	12,157	33.58	49.56	1.81	3.47	3.28	8.30
Newry and Mourne	63,929	33.78	51.36	1.46	3.42	2.96	7.03
Newtownabbey	62,640	28.73	51.44	3.73	3.60	4.63	7.86
North Down	61,170	26.97	50.77	4.87	3.23	5.45	8.72
Omagh	35,553	35.77	50.20	1.28	2.93	2.60	7.21
Strabane	28,291	35.16	50.21	1.32	3.62	2.63	7.06
Health and Social Services Board							
Eastern	517,981	34.01	45.33	3.13	4.30	4.75	8.49
Northern	328,355	30.63	51.04	3.11	3.45	4.19	7.58
Southern	232,369	31.99	51.87	2.04	3.32	3.34	7.44
Western	208,506	36.05	48.32	1.57	3.88	3.30	6.88

KS04

Area	All persons aged 16 and over	Percentage of persons aged 16 and over:					
		Single (never married)	Married	Re-married	Separated (but still legally married)	Divorced	Widowed
Education and Library Board							
Belfast	217,130	41.28	36.94	2.18	5.46	4.86	9.28
North Eastern	304,229	30.43	50.90	3.26	3.49	4.31	7.61
South Eastern	300,851	28.76	51.38	3.81	3.47	4.66	7.92
Southern	256,495	32.10	51.96	1.96	3.29	3.28	7.41
Western	208,506	36.05	48.32	1.57	3.88	3.30	6.88
Parliamentary Constituency							
Belfast East	63,446	30.52	45.24	3.62	4.17	5.58	10.87
Belfast North	66,002	36.28	38.51	2.31	6.30	5.83	10.77
Belfast South	78,391	48.09	35.30	2.12	3.13	3.90	7.46
Belfast West	62,897	40.96	36.60	1.30	8.33	4.62	8.19
East Antrim	65,366	28.33	50.89	4.32	3.70	4.88	7.89
East Londonderry	67,870	32.90	49.48	2.81	3.18	4.46	7.16
Fermanagh and South Tyrone	68,959	34.11	50.92	1.60	2.77	2.61	7.99
Foyle	76,861	37.87	44.80	1.61	5.32	4.17	6.23
Lagan Valley	78,633	28.29	53.07	3.67	3.15	4.43	7.40
Mid Ulster	63,666	34.29	52.34	1.15	2.89	2.42	6.90
Newry and Armagh	75,057	33.77	50.76	1.48	3.50	2.98	7.51
North Antrim	78,407	30.37	51.81	2.71	3.42	3.86	7.82
North Down	68,978	26.66	50.59	4.98	3.27	5.51	8.98
South Antrim	76,788	29.27	52.46	3.74	3.50	4.29	6.72
South Down	77,875	32.56	52.35	2.10	2.96	2.91	7.14
Strangford	76,490	26.85	53.56	4.17	3.18	4.74	7.51
Upper Bann	77,681	30.00	51.11	2.88	3.84	4.50	7.67
West Tyrone	63,844	35.50	50.21	1.30	3.23	2.61	7.15
NUTS Level III							
Belfast	217,130	41.28	36.94	2.18	5.46	4.86	9.28
Outer Belfast	287,017	28.39	51.22	3.97	3.63	4.84	7.96
East of Northern Ireland	304,593	29.72	51.52	3.31	3.49	4.34	7.63
North of Northern Ireland	205,703	34.90	48.09	2.08	4.06	3.94	6.93
West and South of Northern Ireland	272,768	34.03	51.54	1.44	3.00	2.65	7.34

Table KS05: Country of Birth

Area	All persons	Percentage of persons born in:						
		Northern Ireland	England	Scotland	Wales	Republic of Ireland	Other EU countries[1]	Elsewhere
Northern Ireland	**1,685,267**	**91.04**	**3.66**	**1.00**	**0.18**	**2.32**	**0.61**	**1.20**
Local Government District								
Antrim	48,366	87.04	7.30	1.62	0.48	1.35	0.84	1.37
Ards	73,244	92.25	3.71	1.05	0.20	1.20	0.47	1.12
Armagh	54,263	91.66	2.92	0.64	0.11	3.41	0.53	0.73
Ballymena	58,610	93.88	2.78	0.97	0.11	0.89	0.46	0.91
Ballymoney	26,894	94.97	2.62	0.66	0.08	0.86	0.28	0.54
Banbridge	41,392	93.77	2.87	0.69	0.14	1.30	0.41	0.84
Belfast	277,391	91.36	2.95	0.80	0.14	1.96	0.96	1.82
Carrickfergus	37,659	91.37	4.25	1.21	0.19	0.95	0.57	1.46
Castlereagh	66,488	92.10	3.11	0.96	0.16	1.55	0.45	1.67
Coleraine	56,315	90.21	3.95	1.22	0.21	2.35	0.58	1.48
Cookstown	32,581	94.69	2.33	0.56	0.10	1.18	0.32	0.83
Craigavon	80,671	92.85	3.25	0.77	0.13	1.47	0.57	0.96
Derry	105,066	88.15	3.99	1.03	0.14	5.11	0.65	0.93
Down	63,828	91.32	4.50	0.80	0.23	1.62	0.44	1.10
Dungannon	47,735	93.10	2.58	0.50	0.07	2.48	0.48	0.79
Fermanagh	57,527	87.00	4.05	0.62	0.13	7.13	0.37	0.69
Larne	30,832	93.04	3.34	1.31	0.17	0.92	0.40	0.83
Limavady	32,422	89.28	4.26	2.41	0.71	1.68	0.56	1.10
Lisburn	108,694	90.06	5.02	1.10	0.26	1.45	0.87	1.25
Magherafelt	39,780	95.18	2.03	0.57	0.07	1.12	0.30	0.72
Moyle	15,933	91.87	3.57	1.46	0.14	1.52	0.62	0.83
Newry and Mourne	87,058	90.01	3.26	0.60	0.13	4.58	0.59	0.82
Newtownabbey	79,995	93.15	2.99	0.88	0.15	1.08	0.40	1.36
North Down	76,323	86.14	6.23	2.69	0.32	1.96	0.81	1.85
Omagh	47,952	90.77	4.26	0.66	0.16	2.52	0.58	1.04
Strabane	38,248	89.70	2.40	1.15	0.05	6.05	0.27	0.39
Health and Social Services Board								
Eastern	665,968	90.72	3.91	1.11	0.20	1.72	0.78	1.57
Northern	426,965	92.38	3.57	1.03	0.18	1.24	0.48	1.11
Southern	311,119	92.01	3.04	0.65	0.12	2.81	0.53	0.84
Western	281,215	88.70	3.86	1.06	0.19	4.81	0.52	0.85

© Crown copyright 2002

Area	All persons	Percentage of persons born in:						
		Northern Ireland	England	Scotland	Wales	Republic of Ireland	Other EU countries[1]	Elsewhere
Education and Library Board								
Belfast	277,391	91.36	2.95	0.80	0.14	1.96	0.96	1.82
North Eastern	394,384	92.19	3.67	1.07	0.19	1.25	0.50	1.14
South Eastern	388,577	90.26	4.60	1.33	0.24	1.55	0.64	1.39
Southern	343,700	92.26	2.97	0.64	0.12	2.66	0.51	0.84
Western	281,215	88.70	3.86	1.06	0.19	4.81	0.52	0.85
Parliamentary Constituency								
Belfast East	79,261	91.76	3.53	1.07	0.19	1.30	0.57	1.59
Belfast North	86,066	93.62	2.62	0.73	0.11	1.28	0.63	1.01
Belfast South	94,994	86.79	3.97	1.04	0.20	3.43	1.21	3.37
Belfast West	87,610	94.78	1.58	0.38	0.07	1.27	1.12	0.80
East Antrim	84,062	91.83	3.75	1.21	0.19	1.08	0.52	1.43
East Londonderry	88,737	89.87	4.06	1.65	0.39	2.10	0.58	1.34
Fermanagh and South Tyrone	91,127	89.05	3.55	0.58	0.11	5.54	0.42	0.75
Foyle	105,066	88.15	3.99	1.03	0.14	5.11	0.65	0.93
Lagan Valley	101,696	89.74	5.29	1.18	0.28	1.44	0.77	1.31
Mid Ulster	86,496	94.86	2.19	0.56	0.08	1.23	0.33	0.75
Newry and Armagh	100,950	90.35	3.02	0.59	0.11	4.62	0.56	0.75
North Antrim	101,437	93.85	2.86	0.96	0.11	0.98	0.44	0.80
North Down	85,992	86.60	6.07	2.54	0.32	1.91	0.79	1.78
South Antrim	99,810	90.63	4.98	1.19	0.30	1.12	0.57	1.20
South Down	104,658	91.54	3.94	0.73	0.19	2.10	0.50	0.99
Strangford	98,158	92.64	3.39	0.96	0.18	1.19	0.44	1.21
Upper Bann	102,947	92.83	3.29	0.77	0.14	1.48	0.54	0.95
West Tyrone	86,200	90.29	3.44	0.87	0.11	4.09	0.44	0.75
NUTS Level III								
Belfast	277,391	91.36	2.95	0.80	0.14	1.96	0.96	1.82
Outer Belfast	369,159	90.42	4.41	1.36	0.22	1.44	0.65	1.50
East of Northern Ireland	396,943	92.05	3.92	0.99	0.20	1.28	0.52	1.03
North of Northern Ireland	274,878	89.80	3.63	1.24	0.20	3.64	0.54	0.94
West and South of Northern Ireland	366,896	91.26	3.16	0.60	0.12	3.59	0.48	0.80

Note:
1 European Union as defined on Census day (29 April 2001). 'Other EU countries' includes United Kingdom; part not specified and Ireland; part not specified.

KS05

17

Table KS06: Ethnic Group

Area	All persons	Percentage of persons in ethnic group:											
		White	Irish Traveller	Mixed	Indian	Pakistani	Bangladeshi	Other Asian	Black Caribbean	Black African	Other Black	Chinese	Other ethnic group
Northern Ireland	**1,685,267**	**99.15**	**0.10**	**0.20**	**0.09**	**0.04**	**0.01**	**0.01**	**0.02**	**0.03**	**0.02**	**0.25**	**0.08**
Local Government District													
Antrim	48,366	99.16	0.02	0.27	0.11	0.07	0.01	0.01	0.02	0.02	0.02	0.25	0.04
Ards	73,244	99.36	0.02	0.19	0.03	0.01	0.08	0.01	0.01	0.02	0.01	0.21	0.06
Armagh	54,260	99.54	0.15	0.11	0.03	-	-	0.01	0.01	0.01	0.01	0.10	0.04
Ballymena	58,609	99.31	0.13	0.15	0.06	0.06	0.01	0.01	-	0.03	0.02	0.16	0.07
Ballymoney	26,889	99.62	0.06	0.09	0.06	-	-	-	-	0.01	-	0.14	0.01
Banbridge	41,392	99.58	0.06	0.14	0.03	0.02	-	0.01	0.01	0.01	0.01	0.08	0.04
Belfast	277,391	98.63	0.09	0.26	0.16	0.06	0.02	0.03	0.02	0.05	0.03	0.48	0.17
Carrickfergus	37,659	99.29	0.01	0.18	0.06	0.02	0.03	0.02	0.02	0.03	0.01	0.23	0.12
Castlereagh	66,488	98.65	0.03	0.25	0.12	0.07	0.04	0.04	0.02	0.09	0.02	0.61	0.08
Coleraine	56,316	99.11	0.06	0.25	0.15	0.02	0.01	0.02	0.02	0.03	0.02	0.28	0.06
Cookstown	32,585	99.52	0.06	0.10	0.02	0.01	0.01	0.01	-	0.01	0.01	0.22	0.02
Craigavon	80,670	99.00	0.16	0.18	0.11	0.15	0.01	-	0.01	0.02	0.02	0.28	0.07
Derry	105,066	99.10	0.16	0.24	0.20	0.03	0.01	0.00	0.03	0.03	0.02	0.14	0.04
Down	63,826	99.35	0.07	0.20	0.03	0.01	-	-	0.03	0.03	0.05	0.16	0.09
Dungannon	47,735	99.22	0.32	0.14	0.05	0.03	0.01	0.01	0.01	0.02	0.03	0.12	0.05
Fermanagh	57,528	99.42	0.15	0.17	0.04	0.02	0.01	0.01	0.01	0.03	0.03	0.08	0.04
Larne	30,831	99.62	0.02	0.19	0.04	0.01	-	-	-	0.01	0.01	0.07	0.03
Limavady	32,421	99.20	0.08	0.19	0.02	-	-	-	0.02	0.02	0.24	0.10	0.14
Lisburn	108,694	99.26	0.05	0.20	0.09	0.02	0.01	0.01	0.01	0.03	0.02	0.23	0.09
Magherafelt	39,779	99.44	0.07	0.16	0.12	0.01	-	-	0.01	0.01	0.01	0.16	0.03
Moyle	15,932	99.69	0.05	0.09	0.04	-	-	-	0.02	-	-	0.09	0.02
Newry and Mourne	87,057	99.41	0.27	0.11	0.02	0.02	0.00	-	0.01	0.01	0.01	0.11	0.03
Newtownabbey	79,995	99.01	0.03	0.18	0.14	0.08	0.01	0.01	0.01	0.04	0.01	0.40	0.08
North Down	76,323	99.09	0.02	0.29	0.04	0.07	0.04	0.03	0.04	0.03	0.01	0.27	0.05
Omagh	47,949	99.36	0.24	0.10	0.11	0.02	-	-	0.01	0.02	0.01	0.09	0.05
Strabane	38,245	99.50	0.14	0.17	0.11	-	-	-	0.01	0.01	0.02	0.03	0.03
Health and Social Services Board													
Eastern	665,968	98.94	0.06	0.24	0.10	0.04	0.03	0.02	0.02	0.04	0.02	0.36	0.12
Northern	426,965	99.29	0.05	0.18	0.09	0.04	0.01	0.01	0.01	0.02	0.01	0.23	0.05
Southern	311,119	99.32	0.20	0.14	0.05	0.05	0.01	0.00	0.01	0.01	0.02	0.15	0.05
Western	281,215	99.27	0.16	0.19	0.12	0.02	0.01	0.00	0.02	0.02	0.04	0.10	0.05

Area	All persons	Percentage of persons in ethnic group:											
		White	Irish Traveller	Mixed	Indian	Pakistani	Bangladeshi	Other Asian	Black Caribbean	Black African	Other Black	Chinese	Other ethnic group
Education and Library Board													
Belfast	277,391	98.63	0.09	0.26	0.16	0.06	0.02	0.03	0.02	0.05	0.03	0.48	0.17
North Eastern	394,384	99.27	0.05	0.19	0.10	0.04	0.01	0.01	0.01	0.02	0.01	0.23	0.06
South Eastern	388,577	99.15	0.04	0.22	0.06	0.03	0.03	0.02	0.02	0.04	0.02	0.29	0.07
Southern	343,700	99.34	0.19	0.13	0.05	0.05	0.01	0.00	0.01	0.01	0.02	0.16	0.04
Western	281,215	99.27	0.16	0.19	0.12	0.02	0.01	0.00	0.02	0.02	0.04	0.10	0.05
Parliamentary Constituency													
Belfast East	79,261	99.01	0.03	0.24	0.04	0.06	0.00	0.02	0.03	0.04	0.04	0.41	0.09
Belfast North	86,066	99.25	0.05	0.19	0.13	0.02	0.01	0.01	0.01	0.03	0.02	0.17	0.11
Belfast South	94,994	97.35	0.06	0.42	0.31	0.09	0.08	0.06	0.03	0.10	0.02	1.17	0.31
Belfast West	87,610	99.27	0.21	0.15	0.06	0.04	0.00	0.02	0.01	0.05	0.02	0.09	0.07
East Antrim	84,062	99.17	0.02	0.22	0.07	0.02	0.01	0.01	0.01	0.03	0.01	0.33	0.09
East Londonderry	88,737	99.14	0.07	0.23	0.10	0.02	0.00	0.01	0.02	0.02	0.10	0.21	0.09
Fermanagh and South Tyrone	91,127	99.40	0.13	0.16	0.04	0.03	0.01	0.01	0.00	0.02	0.03	0.11	0.05
Foyle	105,066	99.10	0.16	0.24	0.20	0.03	0.01	0.00	0.03	0.03	0.02	0.14	0.04
Lagan Valley	101,696	99.25	0.03	0.20	0.09	0.02	0.01	0.01	0.01	0.03	0.01	0.25	0.10
Mid Ulster	86,496	99.38	0.19	0.13	0.07	0.01	0.00	0.00	0.00	0.01	0.01	0.16	0.03
Newry and Armagh	100,950	99.37	0.29	0.11	0.03	0.02	0.00	0.00	0.01	0.01	0.01	0.12	0.03
North Antrim	101,437	99.45	0.10	0.13	0.06	0.04	0.00	0.00	0.00	0.02	0.01	0.14	0.05
North Down	85,992	99.14	0.02	0.28	0.04	0.07	0.04	0.03	0.04	0.03	0.01	0.26	0.05
South Antrim	99,810	99.21	0.02	0.21	0.14	0.08	0.01	0.00	0.02	0.01	0.02	0.23	0.05
South Down	104,658	99.51	0.07	0.15	0.02	0.02	0.00	-	0.02	0.01	0.03	0.10	0.07
Strangford	98,158	99.21	0.02	0.19	0.06	0.03	0.06	0.01	0.02	0.04	0.02	0.26	0.07
Upper Bann	102,945	99.10	0.15	0.18	0.09	0.12	0.01	-	0.01	0.02	0.02	0.24	0.06
West Tyrone	86,199	99.41	0.19	0.13	0.11	0.01	-	0.00	0.01	0.01	0.01	0.06	0.04
NUTS Level III													
Belfast	277,391	98.63	0.09	0.26	0.16	0.06	0.02	0.03	0.02	0.05	0.03	0.48	0.17
Outer Belfast	369,159	99.06	0.03	0.22	0.09	0.05	0.02	0.02	0.02	0.04	0.01	0.34	0.08
East of Northern Ireland	396,943	99.29	0.08	0.19	0.06	0.05	0.02	0.00	0.01	0.02	0.02	0.19	0.06
North of Northern Ireland	274,878	99.25	0.11	0.20	0.13	0.02	0.01	0.01	0.02	0.02	0.04	0.14	0.05
West and South of Northern Ireland	366,896	99.41	0.20	0.13	0.05	0.02	0.00	0.00	0.01	0.01	0.02	0.12	0.04

Table KS07a: Religion

Area	All persons	Percentage of persons stating religion as:						Percentage of persons with no religion or religion not stated
		Catholic[1]	Presbyterian Church in Ireland	Church of Ireland	Methodist Church in Ireland	Other Christian (including Christian related)	Other religions and philosophies	
Northern Ireland	**1,685,267**	**40.26**	**20.69**	**15.30**	**3.51**	**6.07**	**0.30**	**13.88**
Local Government District								
Antrim	48,366	35.19	27.54	11.71	1.60	6.35	0.34	17.26
Ards	73,244	10.43	38.11	16.56	5.02	9.01	0.28	20.59
Armagh	54,263	45.44	17.25	19.42	2.40	6.41	0.11	8.96
Ballymena	58,610	18.96	44.74	11.73	2.48	8.82	0.25	13.04
Ballymoney	26,894	29.55	38.00	12.36	0.62	8.13	0.08	11.26
Banbridge	41,392	28.60	29.82	17.77	2.09	9.06	0.16	12.51
Belfast	277,391	42.13	16.47	14.16	4.65	5.07	0.60	16.93
Carrickfergus	37,659	6.46	30.27	20.86	8.87	10.42	0.27	22.84
Castlereagh	66,488	15.83	27.03	9.48	7.97	10.40	0.46	18.81
Coleraine	56,315	24.14	30.14	22.72	1.52	6.07	0.34	15.06
Cookstown	32,581	55.18	14.98	6.18	1.24	5.59	0.07	6.77
Craigavon	80,671	41.68	10.94	22.58	5.03	8.14	0.36	11.27
Derry	105,066	70.89	10.26	7.88	0.85	1.77	0.29	8.07
Down	63,828	57.13	14.24	9.26	0.84	4.83	0.11	13.58
Dungannon	47,735	57.35	12.23	6.57	1.90	4.22	0.14	7.60
Fermanagh	57,527	55.52	3.14	24.55	4.75	3.68	0.23	8.13
Larne	30,832	22.25	38.41	12.44	4.20	6.84	0.07	15.79
Limavady	32,422	53.14	19.00	12.59	0.83	3.73	0.09	10.62
Lisburn	108,694	30.07	20.41	21.12	4.14	7.88	0.27	16.11
Magherafelt	39,780	61.52	14.13	11.11	0.49	6.29	0.15	6.31
Moyle	15,933	56.61	16.46	15.12	0.14	2.12	0.10	9.45
Newry and Mourne	87,058	75.89	9.47	4.20	0.41	2.30	0.11	7.62
Newtownabbey	79,995	17.09	30.71	17.18	8.13	8.46	0.34	18.09
North Down	76,323	10.00	30.52	19.16	6.19	8.60	0.41	25.12
Omagh	47,952	65.10	10.69	11.10	1.38	3.11	0.19	8.43
Strabane	38,248	63.09	16.82	11.14	1.24	1.71	0.10	5.90
Health and Social Services Board								
Eastern	665,968	31.80	21.95	16.19	4.75	6.87	0.43	18.01
Northern	426,965	29.07	29.90	15.50	3.52	7.33	0.24	14.44
Southern	311,119	52.57	14.34	15.32	2.41	5.73	0.19	9.44
Western	281,215	63.65	10.78	12.83	1.79	2.60	0.21	8.14

© Crown copyright 2002

Area	All persons	Percentage of persons stating religion as:						Percentage of persons with no religion or religion not stated
		Catholic[1]	Presbyterian Church in Ireland	Church of Ireland	Methodist Church in Ireland	Other Christian (including Christian related)	Other religions and philosophies	
Education and Library Board								
Belfast	277,391	42.13	16.47	14.16	4.65	5.07	0.60	16.93
North Eastern	394,384	26.91	31.13	15.45	3.71	7.47	0.25	15.08
South Eastern	388,577	24.43	25.85	17.65	4.82	8.17	0.31	18.77
Southern	343,700	52.82	14.40	15.41	2.30	5.71	0.17	9.19
Western	281,215	63.65	10.78	12.83	1.79	2.60	0.21	8.14
Parliamentary Constituency								
Belfast East	79,261	7.49	28.98	21.79	9.16	10.69	0.31	21.59
Belfast North	86,066	40.53	18.25	15.13	5.68	4.84	0.35	15.22
Belfast South	94,994	35.63	17.32	14.63	4.93	5.58	1.16	20.75
Belfast West	87,610	76.33	4.64	6.23	1.07	1.38	0.26	10.09
East Antrim	84,062	13.31	32.93	17.89	6.90	8.97	0.26	19.74
East Londonderry	88,737	34.74	26.07	19.02	1.27	5.21	0.25	13.44
Fermanagh and South Tyrone	91,127	52.31	7.63	23.28	3.95	4.34	0.21	8.27
Foyle	105,066	70.89	10.26	7.88	0.85	1.77	0.29	8.07
Lagan Valley	101,696	18.16	25.47	24.54	4.76	9.68	0.29	17.10
Mid Ulster	86,496	62.53	12.94	12.15	0.74	5.20	0.10	6.34
Newry and Armagh	100,950	62.82	11.44	11.74	1.50	3.97	0.10	8.44
North Antrim	101,437	27.68	38.51	12.43	1.62	7.58	0.18	12.00
North Down	85,992	9.20	31.68	19.37	6.25	8.49	0.38	24.62
South Antrim	99,810	26.84	30.18	13.44	4.76	7.20	0.31	17.27
South Down	104,658	61.99	14.79	7.28	0.62	4.62	0.12	10.58
Strangford	98,158	13.10	35.44	17.10	5.00	9.46	0.31	19.59
Upper Bann	102,947	39.77	13.71	22.10	4.41	8.06	0.33	11.63
West Tyrone	86,200	64.21	13.41	11.12	1.32	2.49	0.15	7.31
NUTS Level III								
Belfast	277,391	42.13	16.47	14.16	4.65	5.07	0.60	16.93
Outer Belfast	369,159	18.13	26.93	19.54	6.60	8.87	0.35	19.58
East of Northern Ireland	396,943	31.38	27.60	15.11	3.19	7.65	0.24	14.83
North of Northern Ireland	274,878	53.26	19.35	12.79	0.97	3.51	0.22	9.89
West and South of Northern Ireland	366,896	60.97	11.14	13.97	1.79	4.20	0.14	7.78

Notes:
1 The term Catholic includes those respondents who gave their religion as Catholic or Roman Catholic.

KS07a.

21

Table KS07b: Community Background: Religion or Religion Brought Up In

Area	All persons	Percentage of persons with community background:			
		Catholic[1]	Protestant and Other Christian (including Christian related)	Other religions and philosophies	None
Northern Ireland	**1,685,267**	**43.76**	**53.13**	**0.39**	**2.72**
Local Government District					
Antrim	48,366	38.64	56.65	0.45	4.25
Ards	73,244	12.60	82.52	0.37	4.51
Armagh	54,263	48.70	50.05	0.15	1.10
Ballymena	58,610	20.97	76.31	0.32	2.41
Ballymoney	26,894	31.90	66.24	0.11	1.76
Banbridge	41,392	31.47	66.04	0.23	2.26
Belfast	277,391	47.19	48.59	0.78	3.44
Carrickfergus	37,659	8.66	85.08	0.36	5.90
Castlereagh	66,488	18.26	76.95	0.59	4.21
Coleraine	56,315	27.21	69.40	0.45	2.94
Cookstown	32,581	57.64	41.13	0.10	1.14
Craigavon	80,671	44.68	52.88	0.46	1.98
Derry	105,066	75.37	23.20	0.35	1.09
Down	63,828	61.95	35.49	0.16	2.40
Dungannon	47,735	60.80	38.20	0.17	0.83
Fermanagh	57,527	58.73	39.82	0.28	1.18
Larne	30,832	25.18	71.74	0.12	2.95
Limavady	32,422	56.58	41.57	0.14	1.71
Lisburn	108,694	33.35	62.78	0.36	3.52
Magherafelt	39,780	64.13	34.84	0.20	0.84
Moyle	15,933	60.29	38.29	0.13	1.29
Newry and Mourne	87,058	80.64	18.47	0.13	0.76
Newtownabbey	79,995	19.36	76.21	0.45	3.98
North Down	76,323	12.58	80.49	0.54	6.39
Omagh	47,952	69.07	29.66	0.23	1.03
Strabane	38,248	66.19	33.26	0.14	0.41
Health and Social Services Board					
Eastern	665,968	35.69	59.87	0.56	3.89
Northern	426,965	31.69	64.99	0.32	3.00
Southern	311,119	56.16	42.25	0.24	1.35
Western	281,215	67.47	31.19	0.26	1.07

Table KS07b: Community Background: Religion or Religion Brought Up In (continued)

Area	All persons	Percentage of persons with community background:			
		Catholic[1]	Protestant and Other Christian (including Christian related)	Other religions and philosophies	None
Education and Library Board					
Belfast	**277,391**	47.19	48.59	0.78	3.44
North Eastern	**394,384**	29.54	66.97	0.34	3.16
South Eastern	**388,577**	27.48	67.92	0.40	4.20
Southern	**343,700**	56.30	42.15	0.23	1.33
Western	**281,215**	67.47	31.19	0.26	1.07
Parliamentary Constituency					
Belfast East	**79,261**	9.86	84.62	0.44	5.08
Belfast North	**86,066**	44.93	51.86	0.45	2.76
Belfast South	**94,994**	41.36	52.03	1.53	5.08
Belfast West	**87,610**	82.68	16.22	0.31	0.78
East Antrim	**84,062**	15.75	79.17	0.36	4.72
East Londonderry	**88,737**	37.94	59.23	0.34	2.49
Fermanagh and South Tyrone	**91,127**	55.58	43.05	0.26	1.11
Foyle	**105,066**	75.37	23.20	0.35	1.09
Lagan Valley	**101,696**	20.62	75.02	0.39	3.98
Mid Ulster	**86,496**	65.26	33.73	0.14	0.88
Newry and Armagh	**100,950**	67.16	31.83	0.14	0.87
North Antrim	**101,437**	30.04	67.67	0.23	2.06
North Down	**85,992**	11.68	81.63	0.52	6.17
South Antrim	**99,810**	29.71	65.98	0.41	3.90
South Down	**104,658**	66.34	31.82	0.16	1.69
Strangford	**98,158**	15.37	79.99	0.39	4.25
Upper Bann	**102,947**	42.87	54.67	0.43	2.02
West Tyrone	**86,200**	67.79	31.26	0.19	0.76
NUTS Level III					
Belfast	**277,391**	47.19	48.59	0.78	3.44
Outer Belfast	**369,159**	20.79	74.18	0.46	4.58
East of Northern Ireland	**396,943**	34.41	62.31	0.33	2.96
North of Northern Ireland	**274,878**	56.88	41.32	0.28	1.52
West and South of Northern Ireland	**366,896**	64.55	34.30	0.18	0.96

Notes:
1   The term Catholic includes those respondents who gave their religion as Catholic or Roman Catholic.

KS07b

23

Table KS08: Health and Provision of Unpaid Care

Area	All persons	Limiting long-term illness[1]		General health[3]			All persons who provide unpaid care	Provision of unpaid care[4]		
		Percentage of persons with limiting long-term illness	Percentage of persons of working age[2] with limiting long-term illness	Percentage of persons whose general health was:				Percentage of persons who provide unpaid care:		
				Good	Fairly good	Not good		1-19 hours a week	20-49 hours a week	50+ hours a week
Northern Ireland	**1,685,267**	**20.36**	**17.15**	**70.00**	**19.34**	**10.66**	**185,066**	**59.66**	**15.13**	**25.21**
Local Government District										
Antrim	48,366	17.75	15.67	72.79	18.55	8.65	4,815	61.08	13.40	25.52
Ards	73,244	19.35	15.21	69.75	20.25	10.01	8,987	63.71	13.42	22.87
Armagh	54,263	19.33	16.79	71.58	19.21	9.21	5,650	62.57	14.62	22.81
Ballymena	58,610	17.69	13.98	72.63	19.19	8.18	5,664	61.23	13.93	24.84
Ballymoney	26,894	19.62	16.64	70.89	19.95	9.17	2,526	56.85	15.20	27.95
Banbridge	41,392	18.36	15.37	71.89	19.24	8.87	4,439	62.85	14.53	22.62
Belfast	277,391	24.24	19.61	65.76	19.86	14.38	32,706	55.25	16.79	27.96
Carrickfergus	37,659	18.88	15.02	70.36	19.59	10.05	4,285	64.34	12.32	23.34
Castlereagh	66,488	19.45	14.44	69.91	19.77	10.32	8,499	65.15	12.80	22.05
Coleraine	56,315	18.29	15.07	71.50	19.94	8.56	5,396	62.73	13.18	24.09
Cookstown	32,581	21.97	20.42	68.57	20.06	11.37	3,389	57.33	17.88	24.79
Craigavon	80,671	21.51	19.04	68.25	20.00	11.74	8,876	58.06	15.69	26.25
Derry	105,066	21.61	20.65	69.85	18.15	12.00	11,093	52.93	17.31	29.76
Down	63,828	18.99	16.12	72.12	18.70	9.18	7,019	60.81	14.50	24.69
Dungannon	47,735	21.12	18.66	70.06	19.79	10.15	5,059	57.60	15.95	26.45
Fermanagh	57,527	19.22	15.79	72.22	19.29	8.49	5,711	59.83	15.27	24.90
Larne	30,832	19.02	15.26	70.47	19.90	9.63	3,492	61.71	15.03	23.25
Limavady	32,422	19.05	17.73	72.28	18.52	9.19	2,904	54.75	17.87	27.38
Lisburn	108,694	18.23	15.53	71.96	18.36	9.68	12,409	62.01	14.00	23.99
Magherafelt	39,780	18.45	16.12	71.33	19.53	9.14	3,791	59.88	16.57	23.56
Moyle	15,933	21.18	17.98	69.39	20.84	9.77	1,642	56.82	17.11	26.07
Newry and Mourne	87,058	20.43	18.64	71.83	17.90	10.26	9,085	55.71	16.13	28.17
Newtownabbey	79,995	19.13	14.93	70.14	19.46	10.40	9,259	63.78	13.90	22.32
North Down	76,323	18.53	13.28	71.23	19.70	9.07	9,688	69.26	11.48	19.26
Omagh	47,952	20.45	18.40	71.37	18.66	9.96	4,803	59.94	16.86	23.19
Strabane	38,248	23.42	22.06	67.03	20.23	12.75	3,879	51.46	18.20	30.34
Health and Social Services Board										
Eastern	665,968	21.08	16.88	68.86	19.52	11.62	79,308	60.53	14.69	24.77
Northern	426,965	18.90	15.68	71.02	19.56	9.42	44,259	61.44	14.42	24.14
Southern	311,119	20.35	17.98	70.60	19.14	10.26	33,109	58.75	15.51	25.73
Western	281,215	20.87	19.13	70.49	18.80	10.71	28,390	55.49	17.00	27.51

Table KS08: Health and Provision of Unpaid Care (continued)

Area	All persons	Limiting long-term illness[1]		General health[3]			Provision of unpaid care[4]			
		Percentage of persons with limiting long-term illness	Percentage of persons of working age[2] with limiting long-term illness	Percentage of persons whose general health was:			All persons who provide unpaid care	Percentage of persons who provide unpaid care:		
				Good	Fairly good	Not good		1-19 hours a week	20-49 hours a week	50+ hours a week
Education and Library Board										
Belfast	277,391	24.24	19.61	65.76	19.86	14.38	32,706	55.25	16.79	27.96
North Eastern	394,384	18.64	15.29	71.22	19.52	9.26	40,870	61.78	14.14	24.08
South Eastern	388,577	18.83	14.94	71.08	19.28	9.65	46,602	64.24	13.22	22.54
Southern	343,700	20.50	18.21	70.40	19.23	10.37	36,498	58.62	15.73	25.65
Western	281,215	20.87	19.13	70.49	18.80	10.71	28,390	55.49	17.00	27.51
Parliamentary Constituency										
Belfast East	79,261	23.04	16.99	65.48	21.46	13.06	10,217	61.85	13.84	24.31
Belfast North	86,066	27.53	23.38	61.84	21.45	16.70	10,275	51.36	17.64	31.00
Belfast South	94,994	18.36	13.14	72.07	17.87	10.06	10,203	66.06	12.94	21.00
Belfast West	87,610	26.82	25.21	64.40	19.12	16.48	10,734	44.28	21.05	34.67
East Antrim	84,062	18.58	14.77	70.90	19.42	9.69	9,576	63.71	13.26	23.03
East Londonderry	88,737	18.57	16.06	71.79	19.42	8.79	8,300	59.94	14.82	25.24
Fermanagh and South Tyrone	91,127	19.82	16.59	71.38	19.71	8.91	9,224	59.55	15.15	25.30
Foyle	105,066	21.61	20.65	69.85	18.15	12.00	11,093	52.93	17.31	29.76
Lagan Valley	101,696	17.55	13.98	72.41	18.64	8.95	11,545	65.82	12.74	21.44
Mid Ulster	86,496	20.33	18.41	70.13	19.53	10.34	8,726	57.88	17.37	24.74
Newry and Armagh	100,950	20.60	18.46	70.95	18.76	10.28	10,536	57.89	15.80	26.31
North Antrim	101,437	18.75	15.30	71.66	19.65	8.69	9,832	59.37	14.79	25.84
North Down	85,992	18.99	13.56	70.71	19.94	9.36	10,935	68.64	11.65	19.71
South Antrim	99,810	17.50	14.79	72.40	18.70	8.91	10,754	63.75	13.60	22.64
South Down	104,658	18.87	16.38	72.73	18.30	8.98	11,201	59.86	15.02	25.12
Strangford	98,158	18.55	14.74	70.61	19.76	9.63	11,985	64.50	13.28	22.22
Upper Bann	102,947	20.97	18.45	68.95	19.80	11.25	11,248	58.85	15.50	25.65
West Tyrone	86,200	21.77	20.02	69.45	19.36	11.20	8,682	56.15	17.46	26.39
NUTS Level III										
Belfast	277,391	24.24	19.61	65.76	19.86	14.38	32,706	55.25	16.79	27.96
Outer Belfast	369,159	18.77	14.69	70.88	19.25	9.86	44,140	64.80	13.03	22.17
East of Northern Ireland	396,943	19.16	16.02	70.90	19.45	9.64	43,292	61.21	14.37	24.42
North of Northern Ireland	274,878	20.66	18.81	70.16	19.18	10.66	27,440	55.44	16.48	28.09
West and South of Northern Ireland	366,896	20.09	17.77	71.22	19.03	9.75	37,488	58.74	16.04	25.22

Notes:
1 Limiting long-term illness covers any long-term illness, health problem or disability which limits daily activities or work.
2 Working age population is 16-64 inclusive for men and 16-59 inclusive for women.
3 General health refers to health over 12 months prior to Census day (29 April 2001).
4 Provision of unpaid care: looking after, giving help or support to family members, friends, neighbours or others because of long-term physical or mental ill-health or disability or problems relating to old age.

KS08

Table KS09a: Economic Activity – All Persons

Area	All persons aged 16-74	Percentage of persons aged 16-74:										Percentage of unemployed persons aged 16-74:			
		Economically active					Economically inactive					Aged 16-24	Aged 50 and over	Who have never worked	Who are long-term unemployed[2]
		Employees		Self-employed	Unemployed	Full-time student	Retired	Student	Looking after home/family	Permanently sick/disabled	Other				
		Full-time[1]	Part-time[1]												
Northern Ireland	**1,187,079**	**37.55**	**9.94**	**8.28**	**4.14**	**2.36**	**10.98**	**5.70**	**7.43**	**9.33**	**4.30**	**26.74**	**17.37**	**12.55**	**40.41**
Local Government District															
Antrim	**34,579**	44.62	9.94	8.54	2.99	1.95	9.38	4.20	6.69	8.40	3.29	25.24	17.60	8.32	34.62
Ards	**52,878**	39.82	11.48	9.99	3.20	1.85	12.15	4.23	6.86	7.43	2.98	24.14	22.79	8.44	37.90
Armagh	**37,752**	36.23	10.16	11.10	3.65	1.80	10.17	6.09	7.07	9.35	4.37	26.22	17.21	12.42	45.24
Ballymena	**41,948**	41.30	10.83	9.48	3.06	1.73	11.99	4.40	6.59	6.84	3.77	26.93	19.77	8.25	36.42
Ballymoney	**18,887**	37.09	9.41	11.85	3.70	1.55	10.63	4.86	7.71	8.83	4.37	29.08	18.91	9.74	36.82
Banbridge	**29,283**	41.03	10.06	11.37	2.83	1.75	10.30	4.81	6.34	8.05	3.46	23.98	18.92	6.27	37.83
Belfast	**197,519**	34.06	9.26	4.47	5.41	3.73	11.69	7.54	7.59	11.40	4.85	29.44	15.61	16.25	42.62
Carrickfergus	**26,951**	44.85	11.18	5.63	3.44	2.27	11.78	4.22	6.20	7.35	3.09	27.86	18.03	9.29	35.10
Castlereagh	**47,155**	44.37	11.31	6.40	2.53	2.26	14.40	3.77	5.38	6.99	2.59	21.86	21.36	7.71	33.67
Coleraine	**40,089**	35.49	9.95	9.11	4.16	3.63	12.12	7.20	7.23	7.03	4.10	24.06	20.10	9.18	41.21
Cookstown	**22,417**	32.68	9.00	11.81	3.49	1.92	8.75	6.12	8.66	11.62	5.96	28.10	14.69	13.54	38.70
Craigavon	**56,305**	40.02	9.75	7.02	3.51	2.00	11.01	4.73	6.76	10.92	4.27	22.33	17.47	9.27	41.06
Derry	**72,665**	33.64	8.60	5.62	6.80	2.47	8.52	6.82	9.47	12.68	5.37	28.99	15.13	14.42	45.30
Down	**44,249**	37.11	10.23	11.54	3.69	2.14	10.59	5.54	6.87	8.62	3.68	30.15	17.34	11.70	35.05
Dungannon	**32,835**	33.77	9.48	11.30	3.56	1.91	9.68	5.94	8.38	10.90	5.10	27.05	16.35	13.87	38.36
Fermanagh	**39,898**	34.71	9.31	11.64	5.12	1.66	10.04	6.05	8.20	8.04	5.22	22.22	20.95	13.22	39.50
Larne	**22,086**	41.03	10.39	8.15	3.73	1.63	12.88	4.10	6.64	7.71	3.76	22.11	22.24	8.51	38.40
Limavady	**22,761**	37.40	9.16	9.07	5.08	1.48	7.90	5.45	8.57	9.31	6.57	24.31	13.84	12.11	40.83
Lisburn	**76,476**	41.15	11.09	7.62	3.21	2.38	10.87	4.96	7.29	7.88	3.55	29.07	15.88	13.27	38.07
Magherafelt	**27,424**	36.98	8.92	12.89	3.16	1.45	8.89	6.09	8.04	8.73	4.86	25.40	14.55	10.62	39.84
Moyle	**11,073**	30.79	8.66	13.00	4.80	1.44	12.13	5.89	8.41	9.65	5.25	20.90	17.89	11.11	44.44
Newry and Mourne	**59,568**	31.72	9.40	10.86	4.71	1.77	9.42	6.03	9.65	10.73	5.69	25.89	16.65	13.05	44.29
Newtownabbey	**57,907**	43.55	10.84	5.70	3.04	2.81	12.55	4.91	5.98	7.56	3.04	26.63	19.99	8.12	35.66
North Down	**54,882**	41.30	11.54	8.05	3.13	2.48	13.85	4.85	6.28	5.93	2.57	26.40	22.44	7.73	33.55
Omagh	**33,045**	34.49	8.69	11.59	4.66	1.77	8.95	6.34	7.71	10.43	5.36	25.57	15.64	16.16	40.95
Strabane	**26,447**	31.54	8.59	9.15	5.71	1.40	9.23	5.69	9.09	13.45	6.16	25.12	16.17	17.76	43.07
Health and Social Services Board															
Eastern	**473,159**	38.00	10.36	6.86	4.10	2.86	12.03	5.88	7.02	9.06	3.83	28.25	17.38	13.53	39.64
Northern	**303,361**	39.96	10.14	8.92	3.42	2.22	11.26	5.17	6.96	8.04	3.91	25.75	18.71	9.34	37.82
Southern	**215,743**	36.25	9.73	10.04	3.78	1.85	10.13	5.52	7.80	10.20	4.70	25.06	17.13	11.45	42.16
Western	**194,816**	34.16	8.83	8.75	5.74	1.93	8.93	6.27	8.75	11.06	5.59	26.28	16.27	14.65	42.88

Table KS09a: Economic Activity – All Persons (continued)

Area	All persons aged 16-74	Percentage of persons aged 16-74:										Percentage of unemployed persons aged 16-74:			
		Economically active					Economically inactive					Aged 16-24	Aged 50 and over	Who have never worked	Who are long-term unemployed[2]
		Employees		Self-employed	Unemployed	Full-time student	Retired	Student	Looking after home/family	Permanently sick/disabled	Other				
		Full-time[1]	Part-time[1]												
Education and Library Board															
Belfast	197,519	34.06	9.26	4.47	5.41	3.73	11.69	7.54	7.59	11.40	4.85	29.44	15.61	16.25	42.62
North Eastern	280,944	40.54	10.23	8.69	3.41	2.25	11.46	5.09	6.82	7.75	3.75	25.56	19.04	9.00	37.74
South Eastern	275,640	40.83	11.15	8.58	3.15	2.24	12.27	4.69	6.61	7.37	3.10	26.79	19.55	10.18	35.97
Southern	238,160	35.91	9.66	10.20	3.75	1.86	10.00	5.58	7.88	10.33	4.82	25.32	16.92	11.64	41.86
Western	194,816	34.16	8.83	8.75	5.74	1.93	8.93	6.27	8.75	11.06	5.59	26.28	16.27	14.65	42.88
Parliamentary Constituency															
Belfast East	55,969	40.37	10.78	5.32	3.84	1.90	14.83	3.98	6.39	8.91	3.67	24.44	20.72	10.73	36.62
Belfast North	59,503	31.68	9.84	3.57	6.05	2.12	13.55	4.83	8.88	13.62	5.86	29.58	16.71	14.82	44.87
Belfast South	71,904	39.41	8.13	5.99	3.40	6.42	10.25	11.57	4.74	6.92	3.18	29.91	14.32	11.54	35.43
Belfast West	58,818	27.71	9.64	2.86	7.81	2.69	9.99	6.48	10.96	15.63	6.23	31.31	13.10	21.17	46.65
East Antrim	60,400	43.18	10.67	6.51	3.39	2.44	12.09	4.91	6.20	7.38	3.23	25.67	19.32	9.44	35.89
East Londonderry	62,850	36.18	9.66	9.09	4.49	2.85	10.59	6.57	7.72	7.85	4.99	24.16	17.53	10.38	41.06
Fermanagh and South Tyrone	63,234	34.74	9.49	11.70	4.49	1.73	10.21	5.88	7.85	8.86	5.06	23.36	19.94	13.42	38.76
Foyle	72,665	33.64	8.60	5.62	6.80	2.47	8.52	6.82	9.47	12.68	5.37	28.99	15.13	14.42	45.30
Lagan Valley	72,778	43.56	11.26	8.74	2.35	2.12	11.61	4.33	6.16	6.75	3.13	25.06	19.33	8.70	33.00
Mid Ulster	59,340	34.44	8.92	12.04	3.41	1.73	8.63	6.21	8.77	10.42	5.43	27.05	14.54	12.31	39.71
Newry and Armagh	69,832	33.63	9.63	9.79	4.56	1.81	9.86	6.13	8.50	10.74	5.36	26.01	16.27	13.60	45.49
North Antrim	71,908	38.58	10.13	10.64	3.50	1.64	11.65	4.75	7.16	7.79	4.16	26.25	19.13	9.27	38.23
North Down	61,680	40.80	11.54	8.26	3.19	2.38	14.01	4.76	6.33	6.13	2.61	26.13	22.83	8.24	34.01
South Antrim	71,898	45.21	10.66	7.46	2.81	2.25	10.68	4.20	6.28	7.46	2.99	25.73	19.69	7.52	34.24
South Down	72,072	35.12	9.99	12.89	3.64	1.94	9.97	5.69	7.82	8.82	4.11	27.98	17.61	11.36	38.20
Strangford	70,645	41.41	11.44	9.50	2.96	2.08	12.00	4.21	6.41	7.19	2.81	23.26	22.88	7.61	37.53
Upper Bann	72,091	40.42	9.86	7.36	3.44	1.98	10.92	4.80	6.60	10.48	4.14	23.24	17.22	8.59	40.02
West Tyrone	59,492	33.18	8.64	10.51	5.13	1.61	9.07	6.05	8.32	11.77	5.72	25.34	15.90	16.95	42.00
NUTS Level III															
Belfast	197,519	34.06	9.26	4.47	5.41	3.73	11.69	7.54	7.59	11.40	4.85	29.44	15.61	16.25	42.62
Outer Belfast	263,371	42.66	11.18	6.87	3.06	2.46	12.59	4.64	6.34	7.19	3.01	26.76	19.24	9.68	35.58
East of Northern Ireland	281,328	40.47	10.42	9.39	3.30	1.89	11.18	4.61	6.71	8.43	3.62	25.13	19.30	8.96	37.54
North of Northern Ireland	191,922	34.36	9.03	8.28	5.47	2.30	9.71	6.33	8.61	10.65	5.25	26.73	16.32	13.34	43.23
West and South of Northern Ireland	252,939	34.15	9.33	11.48	4.18	1.76	9.49	6.09	8.36	9.94	5.23	25.43	17.06	13.38	41.57

Notes:
1 For the Census; part-time is defined as working 30 hours or less a week. Full-time is defined as working 31 or more hours a week.
2 'Long-term unemployed' are those who stated that they have not worked since 1999 or earlier.

KS09a

Table KS09b: Economic Activity – Males

Area	All males aged 16-74	Percentage of males aged 16-74:										Percentage of unemployed males aged 16-74:			
		Economically active					Economically inactive					Aged 16-24	Aged 50 and over	Who have never worked	Who are long-term unemployed[2]
		Employees		Self-employed	Unemployed	Full-time student	Retired	Student	Looking after home/family	Permanently sick/disabled	Other				
		Full-time[1]	Part-time[1]												
Northern Ireland	581,232	46.64	2.95	13.58	5.67	2.04	9.19	5.32	1.44	9.71	3.45	25.42	19.18	12.09	41.56
Local Government District															
Antrim	17,508	54.90	2.39	13.69	3.76	1.78	7.68	3.68	0.89	8.72	2.52	25.64	21.70	8.04	35.36
Ards	25,943	50.29	2.42	15.83	4.15	1.63	10.65	4.23	0.94	7.76	2.09	23.03	24.98	8.08	37.14
Armagh	18,914	43.63	3.42	17.78	5.10	1.65	8.07	5.35	1.32	10.05	3.65	25.41	17.63	11.93	46.27
Ballymena	20,581	51.37	2.79	15.60	3.65	1.53	9.95	4.09	0.71	7.32	3.01	25.70	21.17	7.06	38.35
Ballymoney	9,421	45.17	2.63	19.77	4.88	1.09	8.41	4.33	1.25	9.20	3.26	28.04	22.39	9.35	37.17
Banbridge	14,692	50.32	1.95	18.38	3.71	1.50	8.17	4.32	0.91	8.12	2.63	23.30	20.00	6.61	35.78
Belfast	92,638	42.81	3.09	7.31	8.11	3.23	9.78	7.35	2.08	12.12	4.12	28.72	17.09	15.51	44.11
Carrickfergus	13,133	57.28	2.12	8.78	4.83	1.93	10.24	4.49	0.81	7.22	2.29	28.23	19.24	8.36	37.38
Castlereagh	22,526	55.50	2.40	10.12	3.53	2.16	12.52	3.87	0.79	7.08	2.02	22.77	23.27	7.17	32.33
Coleraine	19,112	44.97	3.19	14.68	5.58	2.85	10.40	6.32	1.24	7.66	3.12	22.87	23.15	8.25	42.27
Cookstown	11,191	39.62	2.98	20.03	4.41	1.55	7.03	5.22	1.89	12.50	4.77	25.10	15.59	13.56	42.31
Craigavon	27,704	50.63	2.58	11.52	4.91	1.82	8.96	4.48	1.53	10.27	3.31	20.07	18.82	8.01	42.57
Derry	35,290	41.81	3.53	9.52	9.57	2.13	7.43	6.47	2.32	13.01	4.21	26.33	17.71	14.16	46.89
Down	22,149	44.68	2.74	18.71	4.88	1.96	8.70	5.14	1.05	9.12	3.02	29.54	17.87	11.94	33.33
Dungannon	16,396	41.06	3.12	18.70	4.52	1.64	7.56	5.26	2.17	11.53	4.43	22.67	17.81	12.15	41.16
Fermanagh	20,222	41.42	3.68	18.47	7.04	1.42	8.57	5.10	1.34	8.77	4.19	20.08	22.89	13.27	40.52
Larne	10,940	51.70	2.52	12.71	5.05	1.29	10.88	3.63	0.89	8.47	2.86	22.60	26.22	7.41	40.69
Limavady	11,690	44.96	3.55	15.12	6.75	1.18	6.38	4.74	1.76	9.69	5.87	19.90	17.11	11.03	44.74
Lisburn	37,191	52.40	2.60	12.27	4.17	2.16	9.26	4.81	1.23	8.00	3.09	29.61	18.32	12.77	38.65
Magherafelt	13,925	44.16	2.74	22.05	3.78	1.03	7.10	5.35	1.42	8.80	3.55	22.39	15.94	9.68	39.66
Moyle	5,508	36.33	2.81	21.50	6.35	1.25	9.75	5.21	1.53	10.88	4.39	18.57	20.29	10.29	45.14
Newry and Mourne	29,571	38.63	3.65	18.45	6.66	1.45	7.67	5.28	2.03	11.72	4.45	24.06	17.92	12.23	45.94
Newtownabbey	28,012	55.19	2.66	9.23	4.07	2.52	10.63	4.86	1.02	7.56	2.27	25.88	22.81	7.11	36.40
North Down	26,908	53.06	2.96	12.14	3.93	2.33	12.33	4.91	0.62	5.70	2.02	26.11	24.03	7.76	33.77
Omagh	16,768	40.19	3.55	19.00	6.09	1.42	7.43	5.67	1.38	10.98	4.28	24.19	16.55	15.87	41.63
Strabane	13,299	37.86	3.87	15.70	7.97	1.24	7.60	5.09	2.01	13.85	4.80	21.60	18.11	18.40	42.17
Health and Social Services Board															
Eastern	227,355	47.89	2.81	11.06	5.75	2.54	10.27	5.73	1.41	9.40	3.16	27.85	18.89	13.14	40.45
Northern	149,331	49.73	2.69	14.66	4.44	1.85	9.37	4.73	1.10	8.42	3.00	24.73	21.27	8.53	39.13
Southern	107,277	44.58	3.02	16.57	5.20	1.62	8.12	4.95	1.64	10.53	3.76	23.06	18.28	10.59	43.55
Western	97,269	41.29	3.62	14.53	7.89	1.63	7.57	5.65	1.84	11.49	4.50	23.57	18.51	14.49	44.13

Table KS09b: Economic Activity – Males (continued)

Area	All males aged 16-74	Economically active					Economically inactive					Percentage of unemployed males aged 16-74:			
		Employees		Self-employed	Unemployed	Full-time student	Retired	Student	Looking after home/family	Permanently sick/disabled	Other	Aged 16-24	Aged 50 and over	Who have never worked	Who are long-term unemployed[2]
		Full-time[1]	Part-time[1]												
Education and Library Board															
Belfast	92,638	42.81	3.09	7.31	8.11	3.23	9.78	7.35	2.08	12.12	4.12	28.72	17.09	15.51	44.11
North Eastern	138,140	50.54	2.67	14.23	4.45	1.87	9.56	4.69	1.03	8.09	2.86	24.70	21.72	8.13	38.87
South Eastern	134,717	51.38	2.63	13.63	4.13	2.06	10.60	4.61	0.95	7.52	2.49	26.68	21.32	9.95	35.49
Southern	118,468	44.11	3.01	16.90	5.13	1.61	8.02	4.98	1.67	10.72	3.86	23.23	18.06	10.83	43.45
Western	97,269	41.29	3.62	14.53	7.89	1.63	7.57	5.65	1.84	11.49	4.50	23.57	18.51	14.49	44.13
Parliamentary Constituency															
Belfast East	26,549	51.14	3.14	8.35	5.63	1.76	12.39	4.12	1.45	8.99	3.04	25.15	22.54	10.10	35.32
Belfast North	27,751	41.31	3.11	6.15	9.03	1.97	11.40	4.83	2.46	14.82	4.91	29.06	18.44	13.85	46.35
Belfast South	33,831	46.84	2.61	9.27	4.91	5.33	8.85	11.04	0.90	7.51	2.73	29.36	15.64	10.89	37.18
Belfast West	27,302	36.83	3.35	5.30	12.01	2.44	8.46	6.42	3.44	16.54	5.20	29.86	14.49	20.37	48.49
East Antrim	29,530	54.80	2.30	10.20	4.64	2.08	10.38	4.76	0.82	7.58	2.45	26.00	21.69	8.25	37.98
East Londonderry	30,802	44.96	3.32	14.84	6.03	2.22	8.87	5.72	1.44	8.43	4.17	21.61	20.58	9.43	43.32
Fermanagh and South Tyrone	31,909	41.83	3.46	18.69	6.01	1.49	8.44	5.04	1.42	9.44	4.18	20.28	21.69	13.35	40.30
Foyle	35,290	41.81	3.53	9.52	9.57	2.13	7.43	6.47	2.32	13.01	4.21	26.33	17.71	14.16	46.89
Lagan Valley	35,869	54.47	2.43	13.84	2.90	1.90	9.74	4.17	0.87	6.84	2.85	25.36	22.77	7.68	33.62
Mid Ulster	29,825	41.39	2.90	20.62	4.25	1.33	6.90	5.41	1.96	10.98	4.25	24.21	16.01	11.12	41.56
Newry and Armagh	34,725	40.76	3.69	16.03	6.55	1.64	7.99	5.39	1.82	11.77	4.36	24.23	17.37	12.97	46.88
North Antrim	35,510	47.39	2.75	17.62	4.40	1.37	9.51	4.33	0.98	8.37	3.29	24.79	21.33	8.46	39.53
North Down	30,191	52.53	2.96	12.49	4.02	2.23	12.46	4.74	0.66	5.93	1.99	25.54	24.22	7.91	34.51
South Antrim	35,749	56.26	2.53	12.02	3.61	2.06	8.91	3.97	0.87	7.56	2.20	26.10	23.16	7.05	34.24
South Down	36,154	42.17	2.90	21.47	4.77	1.65	8.07	5.09	1.28	9.34	3.26	27.13	17.91	11.13	37.62
Strangford	34,647	51.91	2.27	15.12	3.89	1.91	10.29	4.29	0.87	7.41	2.06	22.92	25.59	7.49	36.42
Upper Bann	35,531	51.21	2.49	11.97	4.77	1.77	8.87	4.48	1.35	9.90	3.17	21.37	18.71	7.79	40.61
West Tyrone	30,067	39.16	3.70	17.54	6.92	1.34	7.51	5.41	1.66	12.25	4.51	22.87	17.35	17.16	41.90
NUTS Level III															
Belfast	92,638	42.81	3.09	7.31	8.11	3.23	9.78	7.35	2.08	12.12	4.12	28.72	17.09	15.51	44.11
Outer Belfast	127,770	54.20	2.61	10.84	4.05	2.25	10.88	4.64	0.94	7.18	2.41	26.85	21.35	9.10	36.03
East of Northern Ireland	139,517	50.32	2.51	15.15	4.32	1.69	9.28	4.30	1.02	8.62	2.79	24.13	21.15	8.43	37.84
North of Northern Ireland	94,320	42.30	3.38	13.85	7.53	1.88	8.16	5.74	1.83	11.13	4.19	24.12	18.95	13.05	44.54
West and South of Northern Ireland	126,987	41.03	3.38	18.99	5.62	1.46	7.71	5.31	1.67	10.63	4.20	23.27	18.36	12.81	43.08

KS09b

Notes:
1 For the Census; part-time is defined as working 30 hours or less a week. Full-time is defined as working 31 or more hours a week.
2 'Long-term unemployed' are those who stated that they have not worked since 1999 or earlier.

Table KS09c: Economic Activity – Females

Area	All females aged 16-74	Percentage of females aged 16-74:										Percentage of unemployed females aged 16-74:			
		Economically active					Economically inactive					Aged 16-24	Aged 50 and over	Who have never worked	Who are long-term unemployed[2]
		Employees		Self-employed	Unemployed	Full-time student	Retired	Student	Looking after home/family	Permanently sick/disabled	Other				
		Full-time[1]	Part-time[1]												
Northern Ireland	**605,847**	**28.83**	**16.64**	**3.18**	**2.66**	**2.67**	**12.69**	**6.06**	**13.17**	**8.97**	**5.11**	**29.45**	**13.67**	**13.49**	**38.06**
Local Government District															
Antrim	17,071	34.07	17.67	3.26	2.20	2.13	11.12	4.73	12.64	8.08	4.09	24.53	10.40	8.80	33.33
Ards	26,935	29.73	20.21	4.37	2.29	2.05	13.60	4.24	12.56	7.12	3.84	26.09	18.96	9.08	39.22
Armagh	18,838	28.80	16.92	4.40	2.19	1.95	12.28	6.84	12.85	8.66	5.10	28.09	16.22	13.56	42.86
Ballymena	21,367	31.61	18.58	3.58	2.50	1.93	13.96	4.70	12.25	6.38	4.51	28.65	17.79	9.93	33.71
Ballymoney	9,466	29.06	16.16	3.96	2.51	2.01	12.85	5.39	14.13	8.45	5.47	31.09	12.18	10.50	36.13
Banbridge	14,591	31.68	18.23	4.32	1.95	1.99	12.45	5.31	11.81	7.97	4.29	25.26	16.84	5.61	41.75
Belfast	104,881	26.33	14.72	1.95	3.02	4.17	13.37	7.71	12.46	10.77	5.50	31.15	12.09	18.02	39.10
Carrickfergus	13,818	33.04	19.79	2.63	2.11	2.59	13.24	3.96	11.32	7.48	3.84	27.05	15.41	11.30	30.14
Castlereagh	24,629	34.18	19.46	2.99	1.62	2.35	16.12	3.69	9.57	6.91	3.10	20.05	17.54	8.77	36.34
Coleraine	20,977	26.85	16.10	4.03	2.86	4.34	13.68	8.01	12.69	6.45	4.98	26.17	14.67	10.83	39.33
Cookstown	11,226	25.75	15.01	3.62	2.57	2.29	10.47	7.01	15.41	10.73	7.14	33.22	13.15	13.49	32.53
Craigavon	28,601	29.75	16.70	2.67	2.15	2.17	12.99	4.99	11.82	11.55	5.21	27.32	14.47	12.03	37.72
Derry	37,375	25.93	13.39	1.95	4.19	2.79	9.55	7.14	16.21	12.36	6.47	34.72	9.57	15.00	41.86
Down	22,100	29.52	17.73	4.36	2.50	2.31	12.48	5.94	12.70	8.13	4.34	31.34	16.30	11.23	38.41
Dungannon	16,439	26.50	15.82	3.92	2.60	2.17	11.78	6.61	14.57	10.27	5.75	34.66	13.82	16.86	33.49
Fermanagh	19,676	27.82	15.09	4.63	3.15	1.92	11.55	7.03	15.25	7.29	6.27	27.14	16.48	13.09	37.16
Larne	11,146	30.56	18.11	3.68	2.42	1.96	14.84	4.56	12.28	6.95	4.64	21.11	14.07	10.74	33.70
Limavady	11,071	29.42	15.09	2.68	3.31	1.81	9.51	6.21	15.76	8.90	7.31	33.79	6.81	14.44	32.43
Lisburn	39,285	30.50	19.12	3.21	2.31	2.59	12.40	5.10	13.03	7.77	3.98	28.15	11.70	14.13	37.09
Magherafelt	13,499	29.57	15.29	3.44	2.51	1.89	10.73	6.84	14.88	8.65	6.20	30.09	12.39	12.09	40.12
Moyle	5,565	25.30	14.45	4.58	3.25	1.64	14.48	6.56	15.22	8.43	6.09	25.41	13.26	12.71	43.09
Newry and Mourne	29,997	24.91	15.08	3.38	2.78	2.09	11.15	6.77	17.17	9.75	6.92	30.22	13.67	14.99	40.41
Newtownabbey	29,895	32.65	18.52	2.39	2.08	3.09	14.35	4.96	10.62	7.57	3.77	28.02	14.81	9.98	34.30
North Down	27,974	29.98	19.80	4.12	2.37	2.62	15.32	4.79	11.73	6.16	3.10	26.85	19.91	7.69	33.18
Omagh	16,277	28.62	13.98	3.95	3.19	2.14	10.52	7.03	14.23	9.86	6.48	28.27	13.85	16.73	39.62
Strabane	13,148	25.14	13.36	2.53	3.41	1.57	10.87	6.29	16.25	13.04	7.54	33.41	11.58	16.26	45.21
Health and Social Services Board															
Eastern	245,804	28.86	17.35	2.99	2.57	3.16	13.66	6.02	12.21	8.74	4.46	29.08	14.24	14.32	37.96
Northern	154,030	30.50	17.36	3.35	2.43	2.58	13.09	5.59	12.64	7.67	4.79	27.55	14.17	10.78	35.49
Southern	108,466	28.01	16.36	3.58	2.37	2.09	12.10	6.09	13.89	9.87	5.62	29.37	14.65	13.33	39.16
Western	97,547	27.05	14.02	2.98	3.61	2.23	10.29	6.88	15.64	10.62	6.67	32.17	11.39	15.02	40.15

Table KS09c: Economic Activity – Females (continued)

© Crown copyright 2002

Area	All females aged 16-74	Percentage of females aged 16-74:										Percentage of unemployed females aged 16-74:			
		Economically active					Economically inactive					Aged 16-24	Aged 50 and over	Who have never worked	Who are long-term unemployed[2]
		Employees		Self-employed	Unemployed	Full-time student	Retired	Student	Looking after home/family	Permanently sick/disabled	Other				
		Full-time[1]	Part-time[1]												
Education and Library Board															
Belfast	104,881	26.33	14.72	1.95	3.02	4.17	13.37	7.71	12.46	10.77	5.50	31.15	12.09	18.02	39.10
North Eastern	142,804	30.87	17.54	3.33	2.42	2.61	13.30	5.48	12.42	7.43	4.60	27.07	14.26	10.55	35.74
South Eastern	140,923	30.74	19.31	3.76	2.23	2.41	13.87	4.76	12.02	7.23	3.68	27.00	16.42	10.58	36.82
Southern	119,692	27.80	16.24	3.58	2.39	2.11	11.95	6.18	14.04	9.96	5.76	29.76	14.50	13.34	38.49
Western	97,547	27.05	14.02	2.98	3.61	2.23	10.29	6.88	15.64	10.62	6.67	32.17	11.39	15.02	40.15
Parliamentary Constituency															
Belfast East	29,420	30.66	17.67	2.59	2.23	2.03	17.04	3.85	10.86	8.84	4.23	22.83	16.59	12.18	39.57
Belfast North	31,752	23.27	15.73	1.32	3.44	2.24	15.44	4.83	14.48	12.57	6.68	30.77	12.73	17.03	41.48
Belfast South	38,073	32.81	13.03	3.09	2.05	7.38	11.49	12.04	8.14	6.39	3.57	31.07	11.51	12.92	31.71
Belfast West	31,516	19.81	15.09	0.74	4.18	2.90	11.31	6.53	17.47	14.84	7.13	34.93	9.64	23.16	42.07
East Antrim	30,870	32.06	18.68	2.99	2.19	2.79	13.73	5.05	11.35	7.18	3.98	25.00	14.50	11.83	31.66
East Londonderry	32,048	27.74	15.75	3.57	3.02	3.46	12.24	7.39	13.75	7.30	5.79	29.06	11.69	12.20	36.71
Fermanagh and South Tyrone	31,325	27.52	15.62	4.57	2.94	1.98	12.02	6.73	14.40	8.26	5.95	29.78	16.30	13.59	35.54
Foyle	37,375	25.93	13.39	1.95	4.19	2.79	9.55	7.14	16.21	12.36	6.47	34.72	9.57	15.00	41.86
Lagan Valley	36,909	32.95	19.85	3.77	1.82	2.33	13.42	4.48	11.30	6.65	3.41	24.59	14.01	10.28	32.04
Mid Ulster	29,515	27.41	15.00	3.36	2.55	2.12	10.39	7.02	15.66	9.85	6.62	31.83	12.07	14.32	36.60
Newry and Armagh	35,107	26.57	15.50	3.63	2.59	1.98	11.71	6.86	15.10	9.71	6.34	30.47	13.53	15.18	42.02
North Antrim	36,398	29.98	17.32	3.84	2.62	1.90	13.75	5.16	13.20	7.23	5.00	28.65	15.53	10.60	36.10
North Down	31,489	29.55	19.76	4.20	2.39	2.52	15.50	4.78	11.77	6.32	3.20	27.09	20.58	8.76	33.20
South Antrim	36,149	34.28	18.69	2.95	2.02	2.44	12.43	4.43	11.62	7.35	3.78	25.07	13.56	8.36	34.25
South Down	35,918	28.02	17.14	4.26	2.50	2.24	11.88	6.30	14.39	8.29	4.97	29.62	17.04	11.80	39.31
Strangford	35,998	31.31	20.27	4.09	2.06	2.24	13.64	4.13	11.75	6.98	3.53	23.89	17.95	7.83	39.54
Upper Bann	36,560	29.92	17.02	2.87	2.15	2.19	12.92	5.11	11.69	11.04	5.09	27.26	14.01	10.32	38.73
West Tyrone	29,425	27.07	13.70	3.32	3.29	1.88	10.67	6.70	15.13	11.28	6.95	30.65	12.80	16.51	42.21
NUTS Level III															
Belfast	104,881	26.33	14.72	1.95	3.02	4.17	13.37	7.71	12.46	10.77	5.50	31.15	12.09	18.02	39.10
Outer Belfast	135,601	31.79	19.26	3.12	2.12	2.66	14.19	4.63	11.43	7.21	3.58	26.59	15.45	10.73	34.78
East of Northern Ireland	141,811	30.77	18.20	3.71	2.29	2.09	13.04	4.92	12.30	8.25	4.43	26.97	15.89	9.94	36.98
North of Northern Ireland	97,602	26.68	14.49	2.90	3.49	2.71	11.21	6.90	15.15	10.19	6.27	32.19	10.82	13.93	40.51
West and South of Northern Ireland	125,952	27.21	15.33	3.90	2.73	2.06	11.28	6.86	15.10	9.26	6.28	29.90	14.36	14.56	38.45

Notes:

1 For the Census; part-time is defined as working 30 hours or less a week. Full-time is defined as working 31 or more hours a week.

2 'Long-term unemployed' are those who stated that they have not worked since 1999 or earlier.

Table KS10: Hours Worked[1]

| Area | All males aged 16-74 in employ-ment[2] | Percentage of males aged 16-74 in employment: | | | | | | All females aged 16-74 in employ-ment[2] | Percentage of females aged 16-74 in employment: | | | | | | Average (mean) weekly hours worked: | |
| | | Working part-time | | | Working full-time | | | | Working part-time | | | Working full-time | | | | |
		1-5 hours a week	6-15 hours a week	16-30 hours a week	31-37 hours a week	38-48 hours a week	49 or more hours a week		1-5 hours a week	6-15 hours a week	16-30 hours a week	31-37 hours a week	38-48 hours a week	49 or more hours a week	Males	Females
Northern Ireland	**377,391**	**0.30**	**2.37**	**6.09**	**15.42**	**56.00**	**19.82**	**309,253**	**1.45**	**9.36**	**28.06**	**25.03**	**31.72**	**4.38**	**41.98**	**31.83**
Local Government District																
Antrim	12,715	0.13	1.98	4.59	14.63	55.33	23.34	9,723	0.95	8.35	26.71	27.32	31.93	4.74	43.60	32.65
Ards	18,138	0.23	2.07	4.95	16.09	56.54	20.12	15,130	1.36	9.68	31.34	23.37	30.31	3.93	42.31	31.14
Armagh	12,537	0.24	2.13	7.02	12.63	54.31	23.67	9,765	1.41	8.73	27.91	25.86	31.58	4.52	43.25	32.27
Ballymena	14,636	0.28	1.82	5.16	17.40	55.64	19.70	11,863	1.44	9.04	28.18	27.55	29.76	4.03	42.33	31.74
Ballymoney	6,451	0.19	1.63	5.46	10.73	60.35	21.66	4,824	1.72	8.54	27.05	24.27	34.06	4.35	43.27	32.25
Banbridge	10,579	0.27	1.50	4.22	11.43	58.90	23.68	8,179	0.97	9.19	27.86	22.85	34.81	4.32	43.51	32.36
Belfast	51,804	0.50	3.61	7.07	21.06	53.13	14.63	49,022	1.58	10.22	28.22	26.06	29.53	4.40	39.69	31.26
Carrickfergus	9,180	0.20	2.30	3.99	20.13	56.38	17.00	7,996	1.24	8.52	29.88	26.90	29.90	3.56	41.12	31.40
Castlereagh	15,767	0.32	2.37	4.78	20.52	55.20	16.80	14,477	1.15	8.62	28.39	26.58	30.83	4.43	40.94	31.95
Coleraine	12,472	0.26	3.05	6.83	12.44	56.14	21.26	10,684	1.59	12.06	27.85	22.46	31.07	4.97	42.10	31.26
Cookstown	7,169	0.32	2.36	6.57	9.95	56.93	23.88	5,213	1.30	9.73	27.41	23.46	33.40	4.70	43.53	32.22
Craigavon	18,378	0.27	1.90	5.09	14.53	61.30	16.92	14,615	1.20	8.01	28.66	24.28	34.36	3.50	41.46	32.06
Derry	19,945	0.31	2.59	7.70	15.42	58.57	15.41	16,280	1.59	9.91	25.18	25.08	34.61	3.62	40.82	31.87
Down	15,014	0.29	2.26	5.81	15.56	55.02	21.07	11,867	1.55	9.76	27.96	26.21	30.17	4.36	42.36	31.74
Dungannon	10,542	0.18	1.92	6.87	10.62	56.74	23.67	7,919	1.60	8.89	28.21	23.05	33.15	5.10	43.22	32.31
Fermanagh	13,101	0.30	2.11	7.75	10.17	54.64	25.04	9,681	1.35	8.68	26.00	22.02	35.70	6.25	43.59	33.14
Larne	7,436	0.30	1.39	5.03	15.56	56.23	21.50	6,031	1.82	9.14	27.82	24.29	32.07	4.86	42.88	31.90
Limavady	7,550	0.17	1.38	6.29	10.48	59.64	22.04	5,395	1.33	8.40	25.62	21.80	38.81	4.04	43.39	32.67
Lisburn	25,720	0.21	2.37	5.33	15.73	55.52	20.84	21,680	1.34	8.91	30.46	24.19	30.35	4.75	42.11	31.63
Magherafelt	9,731	0.20	1.51	5.65	9.47	58.58	24.59	6,746	1.60	8.54	25.21	26.59	34.05	4.00	43.88	32.63
Moyle	3,401	0.44	1.44	7.06	13.32	53.78	23.96	2,548	1.65	9.11	26.49	26.45	30.22	6.08	43.80	32.54
Newry and Mourne	18,317	0.31	1.89	7.73	10.49	58.68	20.91	13,556	1.73	9.49	27.60	23.07	33.68	4.42	42.43	31.98
Newtownabbey	19,428	0.41	2.62	4.79	19.18	56.32	16.69	16,863	1.30	9.33	28.39	27.43	30.04	3.51	40.95	31.44
North Down	18,885	0.36	2.97	5.91	17.32	53.10	20.34	15,744	1.59	10.21	30.66	23.41	29.74	4.39	41.65	31.10
Omagh	10,719	0.27	2.29	6.92	13.07	50.96	26.50	7,887	1.48	8.95	23.70	28.38	32.00	5.49	44.05	32.95
Strabane	7,776	0.26	2.03	8.41	11.63	57.57	20.10	5,565	1.81	7.94	25.77	22.64	37.45	4.38	42.33	32.67
Health and Social Services Board																
Eastern	145,328	0.36	2.84	5.97	18.38	54.39	18.06	127,920	1.46	9.71	29.26	25.17	29.99	4.40	41.11	31.41
Northern	102,619	0.27	2.14	5.33	15.08	56.50	20.68	82,491	1.41	9.34	27.74	25.97	31.27	4.27	42.47	31.86
Southern	70,353	0.26	1.88	6.25	12.09	58.33	21.19	54,034	1.39	8.82	28.07	23.86	33.58	4.27	42.61	32.16
Western	59,091	0.28	2.20	7.48	12.70	56.32	21.02	44,808	1.52	9.05	25.22	24.30	35.25	4.66	42.55	32.53

KS10

Area	All males aged 16-74 in employment²	Percentage of males aged 16-74 in employment:						All females aged 16-74 in employment²	Percentage of females aged 16-74 in employment:						Average (mean) weekly hours worked:	
		Working part-time			Working full-time				Working part-time			Working full-time			Males	Females
		1-5 hours a week	6-15 hours a week	16-30 hours a week	31-37 hours a week	38-48 hours a week	49 or more hours a week		1-5 hours a week	6-15 hours a week	16-30 hours a week	31-37 hours a week	38-48 hours a week	49 or more hours a week		
Education and Library Board																
Belfast	51,804	0.50	3.61	7.07	21.06	53.13	14.63	49,022	1.58	10.22	28.22	26.06	29.53	4.40	39.69	31.26
North Eastern	95,450	0.27	2.12	5.24	15.46	56.47	20.44	77,278	1.42	9.32	27.76	26.14	31.13	4.24	42.39	31.84
South Eastern	93,524	0.28	2.41	5.36	16.90	55.09	19.96	78,898	1.39	9.39	29.91	24.62	30.28	4.40	41.90	31.51
Southern	77,522	0.27	1.92	6.28	11.89	58.20	21.44	59,247	1.39	8.90	28.01	23.83	33.56	4.31	42.69	32.17
Western	59,091	0.28	2.20	7.48	12.70	56.32	21.02	44,808	1.52	9.05	25.22	24.30	35.25	4.66	42.55	32.53
Parliamentary Constituency																
Belfast East	17,027	0.46	2.57	5.69	21.48	54.37	15.43	15,528	1.41	9.20	28.10	26.28	30.63	4.38	40.40	31.64
Belfast North	14,474	0.26	2.75	6.87	22.74	54.59	12.79	13,424	1.53	8.86	31.82	26.42	28.29	3.08	39.64	30.76
Belfast South	21,455	0.64	4.67	6.43	18.91	51.73	17.62	21,178	1.51	11.47	22.86	25.74	32.39	6.03	40.09	32.27
Belfast West	12,924	0.33	3.03	8.54	22.32	55.04	10.74	12,022	1.73	9.36	34.73	26.62	25.13	2.44	38.85	29.83
East Antrim	20,404	0.30	2.13	4.49	18.05	56.18	18.85	17,381	1.54	9.19	28.51	25.98	30.66	4.13	41.72	31.54
East Londonderry	20,022	0.23	2.42	6.63	11.70	57.46	21.56	16,079	1.51	10.83	27.10	22.24	33.67	4.66	42.59	31.73
Fermanagh and South Tyrone	20,825	0.25	2.04	7.34	10.31	54.93	25.12	15,490	1.47	8.73	26.99	22.11	34.71	5.99	43.64	32.86
Foyle	19,945	0.31	2.59	7.70	15.42	58.57	15.41	16,280	1.59	9.91	25.18	25.08	34.61	3.62	40.82	31.87
Lagan Valley	25,982	0.21	2.11	4.91	14.90	55.65	22.21	21,677	1.25	8.67	29.64	23.98	31.45	5.01	42.61	32.00
Mid Ulster	19,718	0.24	1.88	6.25	9.83	58.23	23.58	14,069	1.47	9.06	26.31	25.23	33.71	4.24	43.47	32.39
Newry and Armagh	21,492	0.27	2.11	7.81	12.26	56.30	21.25	16,654	1.52	8.80	27.70	25.12	32.53	4.33	42.47	32.18
North Antrim	24,488	0.28	1.72	5.50	15.08	56.62	20.81	19,235	1.54	8.93	27.67	26.58	30.90	4.38	42.78	31.98
North Down	21,106	0.35	2.89	5.93	16.98	53.59	20.27	17,571	1.60	10.24	30.82	23.39	29.55	4.40	41.68	31.06
South Antrim	25,996	0.27	2.25	4.62	16.85	55.91	20.10	21,026	1.08	8.65	27.76	27.53	30.95	4.04	42.34	32.06
South Down	24,563	0.29	1.93	6.10	12.67	55.84	23.15	18,472	1.59	9.89	27.80	24.62	31.50	4.61	43.13	31.87
Strangford	24,581	0.27	2.26	4.75	17.08	56.24	19.39	20,777	1.28	9.32	30.67	24.19	30.46	4.09	41.97	31.40
Upper Bann	23,894	0.27	1.82	4.88	13.96	61.35	17.72	18,938	1.10	8.46	28.59	23.85	34.51	3.49	41.69	32.03
West Tyrone	18,495	0.26	2.18	7.55	12.46	53.74	23.81	13,452	1.62	8.53	24.55	26.00	34.26	5.03	43.33	32.83
NUTS Level III																
Belfast	51,804	0.50	3.61	7.07	21.06	53.13	14.63	49,022	1.58	10.22	28.22	26.06	29.53	4.40	39.69	31.26
Outer Belfast	88,980	0.30	2.54	5.10	18.12	55.21	18.72	76,760	1.34	9.17	29.59	25.47	30.20	4.22	41.45	31.52
East of Northern Ireland	96,896	0.25	1.90	5.02	15.17	57.14	20.52	77,408	1.31	9.02	28.61	25.13	31.78	4.15	42.50	31.88
North of Northern Ireland	57,595	0.27	2.28	7.13	12.96	57.97	19.39	45,296	1.60	9.80	26.21	23.76	34.32	4.30	42.09	32.00
West and South of Northern Ireland	82,116	0.26	2.01	7.06	10.95	55.95	23.77	60,767	1.52	9.00	26.69	24.46	33.39	4.93	43.32	32.47

Notes:
1 Hours worked is the average number of hours worked a week for the last four weeks before the Census (29 April 2001).
2 'In employment' includes economically active full time students in employment.

Table KS11a: Industry of Employment – All Persons

Area	All persons aged 16-74 in employment	Percentage of persons aged 16-74 in employment working in:												
		Agriculture, hunting, forestry and fishing	Manufacturing	Electricity, gas and water supply	Mining & quarrying and construction	Wholesale & retail trade, repair of motor vehicles	Hotels and catering	Transport, storage and communication	Financial intermediation	Real estate, renting and business activities	Public administration and defence	Education	Health and social work	Other[1]
Northern Ireland	**686,644**	**3.02**	**14.18**	**0.70**	**9.37**	**16.71**	**4.52**	**5.42**	**2.97**	**7.84**	**9.32**	**8.81**	**12.74**	**4.41**
Local Government District														
Antrim	22,438	3.31	13.94	0.62	8.84	13.23	5.17	7.47	2.30	6.90	13.70	6.61	14.68	3.23
Ards	33,268	3.40	13.26	0.62	9.11	17.06	4.02	4.54	3.78	8.21	12.17	6.52	12.43	4.86
Armagh	22,302	6.04	14.00	0.55	11.25	17.13	3.43	5.15	2.04	5.76	8.98	8.38	13.56	3.72
Ballymena	26,499	4.36	17.92	0.96	10.22	18.70	4.37	4.54	2.15	6.31	6.84	7.99	12.00	3.63
Ballymoney	11,275	6.36	17.79	0.49	14.55	17.02	3.74	4.63	1.72	5.55	6.16	6.92	11.76	3.32
Banbridge	18,758	4.79	16.32	0.71	12.27	16.33	3.77	4.92	2.47	6.46	9.83	6.93	11.47	3.72
Belfast	100,826	0.32	10.49	0.63	5.24	16.36	5.65	6.69	3.81	11.68	8.06	10.09	14.89	6.08
Carrickfergus	17,176	0.69	16.14	1.21	5.88	16.80	4.34	8.19	4.41	8.41	9.99	8.14	11.38	4.42
Castlereagh	30,244	0.78	11.36	0.71	5.22	15.99	3.67	5.59	5.08	10.20	11.55	9.21	15.79	4.85
Coleraine	23,156	3.58	13.05	0.46	8.47	19.26	6.56	3.36	1.94	6.46	9.48	11.56	11.27	4.55
Cookstown	12,382	6.53	17.45	0.53	14.62	17.86	4.39	3.71	1.97	4.98	5.78	8.57	10.14	3.45
Craigavon	32,993	2.08	23.25	0.71	8.34	17.74	4.12	4.98	2.26	6.80	7.96	7.31	10.93	3.52
Derry	36,225	1.34	16.20	0.84	7.83	16.46	5.06	4.73	1.90	8.68	8.40	11.06	13.23	4.28
Down	26,881	3.75	9.38	0.58	13.59	14.75	4.81	3.78	2.67	6.79	10.65	9.16	15.24	4.85
Dungannon	18,461	6.36	19.06	0.47	12.23	16.32	3.70	4.42	1.71	5.67	6.15	9.31	11.33	3.28
Fermanagh	22,782	7.35	14.61	0.59	13.06	15.77	4.81	4.52	2.03	4.68	7.57	8.83	12.26	3.92
Larne	13,467	3.24	18.31	2.10	7.80	15.11	4.56	9.44	2.73	6.42	7.80	7.48	10.77	4.23
Limavady	12,945	4.30	16.33	0.87	15.03	13.53	4.47	3.13	1.48	5.47	14.43	7.84	10.22	2.89
Lisburn	47,400	1.87	13.15	0.55	6.91	18.51	4.11	5.30	3.61	8.39	12.29	8.18	12.64	4.47
Magherafelt	16,477	5.87	16.84	0.52	18.82	14.32	3.53	3.82	2.08	4.87	5.80	8.85	11.76	2.93
Moyle	5,949	7.73	10.29	0.66	16.79	13.40	6.15	4.47	1.65	5.92	5.46	9.78	12.71	4.99
Newry and Mourne	31,873	4.36	13.17	0.55	16.27	17.54	3.87	5.10	2.40	5.87	5.45	9.48	11.68	4.26
Newtownabbey	36,291	0.92	14.27	0.81	6.23	19.44	3.85	8.95	4.30	8.73	8.34	8.65	11.15	4.36
North Down	34,629	0.63	11.44	0.66	4.94	16.47	4.76	5.17	4.45	10.16	15.38	8.46	12.35	5.13
Omagh	18,606	6.45	10.27	0.84	14.23	15.51	3.86	3.62	2.03	6.05	9.60	10.29	13.79	3.46
Strabane	13,341	7.08	19.23	0.64	13.85	15.65	3.82	3.66	1.60	4.76	7.56	8.44	9.98	3.72
Health and Social Services Board														
Eastern	273,248	1.39	11.40	0.62	6.78	16.63	4.77	5.59	3.88	9.85	10.86	8.93	14.01	5.28
Northern	185,110	3.55	15.59	0.83	10.01	17.10	4.60	6.19	2.75	6.80	8.41	8.48	11.78	3.91
Southern	124,387	4.42	17.34	0.60	12.06	17.16	3.82	4.95	2.21	6.16	7.51	8.30	11.74	3.74
Western	103,899	4.68	15.19	0.77	11.80	15.67	4.56	4.15	1.86	6.43	9.08	9.69	12.32	3.81

Percentage of persons aged 16-74 in employment working in:

Area	All persons aged 16-74 in employment	Agriculture, hunting, forestry and fishing	Manufac-turing	Electricity, gas and water supply	Mining & quarrying and construction	Wholesale & retail trade, repair of motor vehicles	Hotels and catering	Transport, storage and communic-ation	Financial intermed-iation	Real estate, renting and business activities	Public adminis-tration and defence	Education	Health and social work	Other[1]
Education and Library Board														
Belfast	100,826	0.32	10.49	0.63	5.24	16.36	5.65	6.69	3.81	11.68	8.06	10.09	14.89	6.08
North Eastern	172,728	3.33	15.46	0.85	9.68	17.04	4.61	6.37	2.81	6.93	8.60	8.48	11.90	3.94
South Eastern	172,422	2.02	11.93	0.62	7.68	16.79	4.26	4.94	3.92	8.78	12.50	8.25	13.50	4.81
Southern	136,769	4.61	17.35	0.60	12.29	17.22	3.87	4.84	2.18	6.05	7.36	8.32	11.59	3.71
Western	103,899	4.68	15.19	0.77	11.80	15.67	4.56	4.15	1.86	6.43	9.08	9.69	12.32	3.81
Parliamentary Constituency														
Belfast East	32,555	0.44	11.85	0.70	5.03	16.48	4.29	6.39	4.55	11.58	10.89	8.89	13.18	5.74
Belfast North	27,898	0.25	12.28	0.66	6.25	18.28	5.30	8.46	3.26	9.86	7.13	8.98	13.43	5.85
Belfast South	42,633	0.36	8.88	0.65	3.68	14.76	6.02	5.18	4.37	14.09	7.99	12.10	16.03	5.88
Belfast West	24,946	0.26	11.11	0.51	7.16	17.91	5.90	7.64	3.23	7.88	7.25	8.77	16.50	5.86
East Antrim	37,785	1.56	16.58	1.47	6.46	16.27	4.45	8.66	3.80	7.78	8.81	8.64	11.18	4.35
East Londonderry	36,101	3.84	14.22	0.61	10.83	17.21	5.81	3.28	1.78	6.11	11.25	10.23	10.89	3.95
Fermanagh and South Tyrone	36,315	7.21	16.34	0.56	12.12	16.13	4.45	4.56	1.87	5.01	7.13	8.96	11.99	3.67
Foyle	36,225	1.34	16.20	0.84	7.83	16.46	5.06	4.73	1.90	8.68	8.40	11.06	13.23	4.28
Lagan Valley	47,659	2.32	13.39	0.60	7.46	18.12	3.75	5.11	3.62	8.29	12.54	7.92	12.57	4.31
Mid Ulster	33,787	5.94	17.31	0.50	16.99	15.75	3.82	3.78	2.03	5.07	5.75	8.86	11.02	3.19
Newry and Armagh	38,146	4.95	13.42	0.60	12.42	17.82	3.74	5.17	2.24	5.80	7.55	9.13	13.09	4.06
North Antrim	43,723	5.33	16.85	0.80	12.23	17.55	4.45	4.56	1.97	6.06	6.47	7.95	12.04	3.73
North Down	38,677	0.91	11.69	0.64	5.29	16.42	4.77	5.11	4.32	10.01	14.92	8.30	12.46	5.16
South Antrim	47,022	2.17	13.84	0.74	7.67	16.68	4.29	8.31	3.49	7.79	11.14	7.36	12.78	3.75
South Down	43,035	4.97	10.74	0.50	15.98	15.42	4.31	4.37	2.40	6.19	8.37	8.81	13.51	4.44
Strangford	45,358	2.91	13.01	0.62	8.58	16.68	3.78	4.63	4.10	8.45	12.15	6.97	13.35	4.78
Upper Bann	42,832	2.11	22.36	0.73	8.62	17.56	4.17	4.95	2.25	6.83	8.66	7.31	10.83	3.60
West Tyrone	31,947	6.71	14.01	0.76	14.07	15.57	3.84	3.64	1.85	5.51	8.75	9.52	12.20	3.57
NUTS Level III														
Belfast	100,826	0.32	10.49	0.63	5.24	16.36	5.65	6.69	3.81	11.68	8.06	10.09	14.89	6.08
Outer Belfast	165,740	1.08	13.02	0.73	5.93	17.65	4.13	6.43	4.29	9.17	11.70	8.53	12.70	4.65
East of Northern Ireland	174,304	3.48	16.07	0.81	10.03	16.36	4.38	5.30	2.66	6.94	9.94	7.43	12.57	4.04
North of Northern Ireland	102,891	3.88	15.73	0.69	10.92	16.50	5.08	4.06	1.78	6.76	8.88	9.90	11.80	4.03
West and South of Northern Ireland	142,883	5.99	14.71	0.58	14.34	16.43	3.93	4.47	2.07	5.47	7.04	9.14	12.17	3.67

KS11a

Note:
1   Other includes: other community, social and personal service activities, private households with employed persons and extra-territorial organisations and bodies.

Table KS11b: Industry of Employment – Males

Area	All males aged 16-74 in employment	Percentage of males aged 16-74 in employment working in:												
		Agriculture, hunting, forestry and fishing	Manufacturing	Electricity, gas and water supply	Mining & quarrying and construction	Wholesale & retail trade, repair of motor vehicles	Hotels and catering	Transport, storage and communication	Financial intermediation	Real estate, renting and business activities	Public administration and defence	Education	Health and social work	Other[1]
Northern Ireland	**377,391**	**4.72**	**19.17**	**1.04**	**15.86**	**15.85**	**3.28**	**7.30**	**2.16**	**7.95**	**9.96**	**4.79**	**4.15**	**3.76**
Local Government District														
Antrim	12,715	4.87	17.55	0.92	14.32	12.42	3.55	9.75	1.67	6.77	17.34	3.30	4.77	2.76
Ards	18,138	5.27	19.02	0.89	15.55	16.24	2.96	6.01	2.68	8.14	12.87	3.25	3.26	3.86
Armagh	12,537	9.16	17.99	0.79	18.97	16.93	2.08	7.22	1.31	5.56	9.21	3.83	3.72	3.22
Ballymena	14,636	6.48	24.04	1.43	17.14	17.31	2.96	6.36	1.46	6.03	6.63	3.81	3.07	3.29
Ballymoney	6,451	9.56	21.02	0.70	24.12	15.64	1.98	6.51	0.96	5.57	5.41	2.91	2.87	2.74
Banbridge	10,579	7.20	20.97	1.11	20.13	14.97	2.53	6.62	1.68	6.35	10.03	2.92	2.54	2.94
Belfast	51,804	0.51	15.92	0.91	9.37	15.84	4.99	9.72	3.16	12.63	8.08	6.67	6.65	5.56
Carrickfergus	9,180	1.03	22.77	2.04	9.91	15.86	3.15	10.49	3.09	8.98	11.46	4.67	2.81	3.74
Castlereagh	15,767	1.28	17.20	1.08	9.01	16.64	3.29	7.59	4.33	11.14	12.46	5.69	6.18	4.10
Coleraine	12,472	5.63	16.90	0.71	14.62	17.98	4.55	4.90	1.46	7.05	11.08	7.27	3.46	4.39
Cookstown	7,169	9.83	23.35	0.85	23.70	16.59	2.33	4.95	1.16	4.55	5.01	3.29	1.72	2.68
Craigavon	18,378	3.25	29.66	1.04	13.88	16.90	2.70	6.57	1.57	6.41	8.06	3.74	3.27	2.93
Derry	19,945	2.15	21.79	1.30	13.24	14.69	3.79	6.41	1.34	8.88	9.19	7.01	6.09	4.13
Down	15,014	5.73	12.99	0.85	23.13	14.89	3.67	4.88	1.92	6.69	11.19	4.78	5.27	4.02
Dungannon	10,542	9.52	24.91	0.71	20.27	15.89	2.16	6.00	1.08	5.16	4.92	4.09	2.65	2.63
Fermanagh	13,101	11.21	18.56	0.86	21.35	14.51	2.96	5.36	1.24	4.59	8.33	4.30	3.36	3.39
Larne	7,436	4.72	23.94	3.28	13.11	13.66	2.95	12.22	1.90	6.44	7.96	3.67	2.50	3.64
Limavady	7,550	6.60	18.69	1.34	24.44	11.21	2.69	3.80	0.90	5.27	17.23	3.28	2.52	2.04
Lisburn	25,720	2.85	18.10	0.85	11.50	17.64	3.19	7.34	2.86	8.87	14.27	4.75	4.16	3.63
Magherafelt	9,731	8.94	22.06	0.74	29.68	13.34	1.78	5.19	1.15	4.62	4.49	3.68	2.34	1.98
Moyle	3,401	11.97	12.35	0.94	28.08	13.29	3.50	5.79	1.12	6.09	4.85	5.09	2.71	4.23
Newry and Mourne	18,317	6.79	16.89	0.82	26.73	16.31	2.40	7.04	1.52	5.64	4.62	4.36	3.17	3.72
Newtownabbey	19,428	1.38	20.81	1.24	10.39	18.48	2.81	11.80	3.02	8.79	8.85	5.27	3.61	3.56
North Down	18,885	0.95	16.30	1.03	8.01	15.85	4.12	6.68	3.67	11.08	18.96	4.63	3.97	4.76
Omagh	10,719	9.70	13.41	1.05	23.47	15.23	2.56	4.74	1.22	5.71	10.56	4.84	4.94	2.56
Strabane	7,776	10.97	20.83	0.90	22.65	14.43	2.47	5.18	0.87	4.51	6.98	4.30	2.87	3.03
Health and Social Services Board														
Eastern	145,328	2.20	16.58	0.93	11.72	16.20	3.98	7.71	3.11	10.43	11.98	5.34	5.24	4.58
Northern	102,619	5.44	20.82	1.26	16.72	15.95	3.01	8.21	1.87	6.80	8.99	4.45	3.18	3.31
Southern	70,353	6.76	22.24	0.90	20.03	16.31	2.41	6.73	1.45	5.86	7.20	3.85	3.12	3.14
Western	59,091	7.26	19.03	1.11	19.56	14.27	3.07	5.38	1.18	6.32	9.98	5.18	4.40	3.27

Area	All males aged 16-74 in employment	Agriculture, hunting, forestry and fishing	Manufacturing	Electricity, gas and water supply	Mining & quarrying and construction	Wholesale & retail trade, repair of motor vehicles	Hotels and catering	Transport, storage and communication	Financial intermediation	Real estate, renting and business activities	Public administration and defence	Education	Health and social work	Other[1]
Education and Library Board														
Belfast	51,804	0.51	15.92	0.91	9.37	15.84	4.99	9.72	3.16	12.63	8.08	6.67	6.65	5.56
North Eastern	95,450	5.11	20.63	1.29	16.19	15.90	3.06	8.45	1.92	6.97	9.29	4.54	3.29	3.35
South Eastern	93,524	3.13	16.94	0.93	13.03	16.40	3.43	6.60	3.09	9.21	14.14	4.60	4.47	4.04
Southern	77,522	7.04	22.34	0.90	20.37	16.33	2.40	6.56	1.43	5.74	6.99	3.80	2.99	3.10
Western	59,091	7.26	19.03	1.11	19.56	14.27	3.07	5.38	1.18	6.32	9.98	5.18	4.40	3.27
Parliamentary Constituency														
Belfast East	17,027	0.68	17.62	1.06	8.66	16.52	3.43	8.89	3.95	12.52	11.36	5.51	4.88	4.92
Belfast North	14,474	0.41	18.52	0.96	11.29	17.38	4.23	12.01	2.35	10.00	6.97	5.47	5.11	5.32
Belfast South	21,455	0.62	13.29	0.93	6.54	14.56	5.56	7.42	4.02	16.53	8.37	8.58	8.01	5.58
Belfast West	12,924	0.45	17.80	0.73	12.98	16.92	5.59	11.57	2.21	6.99	6.65	6.04	7.26	4.82
East Antrim	20,404	2.32	22.89	2.33	10.89	15.11	3.09	11.17	2.76	8.08	9.71	4.91	3.00	3.73
East Londonderry	20,022	5.99	17.58	0.94	18.32	15.43	3.85	4.49	1.25	6.38	13.40	5.77	3.10	3.51
Fermanagh and South Tyrone	20,825	10.92	20.85	0.85	19.98	15.27	2.70	5.74	1.18	4.84	7.27	4.19	3.15	3.07
Foyle	19,945	2.15	21.79	1.30	13.24	14.69	3.79	6.41	1.34	8.88	9.19	7.01	6.09	4.13
Lagan Valley	25,982	3.54	18.04	0.93	12.21	17.30	2.82	6.96	2.88	8.91	14.58	4.39	3.92	3.52
Mid Ulster	19,718	8.99	23.01	0.74	27.19	14.62	2.00	5.07	1.14	4.64	4.53	3.63	2.09	2.36
Newry and Armagh	21,492	7.59	17.36	0.90	20.85	17.42	2.29	7.31	1.45	5.63	7.40	4.29	3.78	3.73
North Antrim	24,488	8.05	21.62	1.17	20.50	16.31	2.78	6.32	1.28	5.91	6.06	3.75	2.96	3.28
North Down	21,106	1.36	16.81	1.01	8.65	15.74	4.05	6.57	3.52	10.87	18.23	4.54	3.91	4.75
South Antrim	25,996	3.23	18.75	1.15	12.52	15.86	3.09	10.94	2.38	7.74	13.19	3.95	4.10	3.11
South Down	24,563	7.60	14.20	0.72	26.56	14.70	3.01	5.79	1.62	5.93	8.15	4.21	3.98	3.52
Strangford	24,581	4.54	18.67	0.90	14.67	16.36	2.97	6.04	3.01	8.47	12.83	3.56	4.05	3.91
Upper Bann	23,894	3.25	28.61	1.08	14.41	16.49	2.77	6.57	1.58	6.53	8.93	3.63	3.17	2.98
West Tyrone	18,495	10.24	16.53	0.99	23.13	14.90	2.52	4.93	1.08	5.21	9.06	4.61	4.07	2.76
NUTS Level III														
Belfast	51,804	0.51	15.92	0.91	9.37	15.84	4.99	9.72	3.16	12.63	8.08	6.67	6.65	5.56
Outer Belfast	88,980	1.66	18.63	1.14	9.91	17.08	3.32	8.54	3.35	9.74	13.47	5.00	4.22	3.95
East of Northern Ireland	96,896	5.26	21.26	1.21	16.80	15.48	3.05	7.03	1.87	6.76	10.65	3.67	3.61	3.36
North of Northern Ireland	57,595	6.09	19.55	1.03	18.37	14.94	3.41	5.55	1.19	6.88	9.68	5.64	4.06	3.61
West and South of Northern Ireland	82,116	9.11	19.08	0.83	23.52	15.59	2.35	5.96	1.27	5.19	6.75	4.12	3.22	3.00

Percentage of males aged 16-74 in employment working in:

Note:

1 Other includes: other community, social and personal service activities, private households with employed persons and extra-territorial organisations and bodies.

KS11b

Table KS11c: Industry of Employment – Females

Area	All females aged 16-74 in employment	Percentage of females aged 16-74 in employment working in:												
		Agriculture, hunting, forestry and fishing	Manufacturing	Electricity, gas and water supply	Mining & quarrying and construction	Wholesale & retail trade, repair of motor vehicles	Hotels and catering	Transport, storage and communication	Financial intermediation	Real estate, renting and business activities	Public administration and defence	Education	Health and social work	Other[1]
Northern Ireland	**309,253**	**0.94**	**8.09**	**0.27**	**1.45**	**17.76**	**6.03**	**3.13**	**3.95**	**7.71**	**8.54**	**13.71**	**23.23**	**5.19**
Local Government District														
Antrim	9,723	1.28	9.20	0.24	1.68	14.30	7.30	4.49	3.12	7.07	8.93	10.93	27.64	3.84
Ards	15,130	1.16	6.36	0.28	1.40	18.05	5.29	2.79	5.10	8.29	11.34	10.44	23.42	6.07
Armagh	9,765	2.04	8.87	0.24	1.33	17.40	5.17	2.50	2.99	6.02	8.67	14.21	26.20	4.36
Ballymena	11,863	1.74	10.38	0.39	1.69	20.42	6.12	2.30	2.99	6.67	7.10	13.13	23.03	4.04
Ballymoney	4,824	2.07	13.47	0.21	1.74	18.86	6.09	2.11	2.74	5.53	7.15	12.27	23.65	4.08
Banbridge	8,179	1.68	10.32	0.20	2.10	18.08	5.38	2.73	3.50	6.59	9.57	12.12	23.02	4.72
Belfast	49,022	0.12	4.76	0.33	0.88	16.92	6.35	3.50	4.50	10.67	8.05	13.70	23.60	6.62
Carrickfergus	7,996	0.30	8.53	0.25	1.25	17.87	5.72	5.54	5.93	7.75	8.30	12.12	21.22	5.22
Castlereagh	14,477	0.23	5.01	0.30	1.09	15.28	4.09	3.42	5.89	9.17	10.56	13.04	26.26	5.66
Coleraine	10,684	1.18	8.55	0.17	1.29	20.76	8.92	1.57	2.50	5.77	7.61	16.57	20.39	4.73
Cookstown	5,213	2.00	9.34	0.10	2.13	19.62	7.23	2.00	3.09	5.58	6.85	15.83	21.73	4.51
Craigavon	14,615	0.61	15.20	0.29	1.38	18.80	5.91	2.98	3.11	7.29	7.82	11.80	20.55	4.26
Derry	16,280	0.34	9.34	0.29	1.21	18.62	6.63	2.68	2.57	8.43	7.44	16.03	21.97	4.47
Down	11,867	1.24	4.82	0.23	1.53	14.57	6.26	2.39	3.62	6.91	9.98	14.69	27.85	5.92
Dungannon	7,919	2.16	11.28	0.14	1.52	16.88	5.75	2.31	2.54	6.35	7.79	16.25	22.89	4.14
Fermanagh	9,681	2.13	9.28	0.22	1.85	17.48	7.31	3.39	3.11	4.81	6.54	14.96	24.30	4.64
Larne	6,031	1.41	11.37	0.65	1.26	16.90	6.55	6.00	3.76	6.40	7.61	12.17	20.97	4.94
Limavady	5,395	1.09	13.03	0.22	1.87	16.79	6.95	2.19	2.30	5.75	10.51	14.22	21.00	4.08
Lisburn	21,680	0.71	7.27	0.21	1.46	19.55	5.21	2.88	4.51	7.83	9.95	12.25	22.70	5.48
Magherafelt	6,746	1.45	9.29	0.21	3.16	15.73	6.05	1.85	3.41	5.22	7.68	16.32	25.33	4.30
Moyle	2,548	2.08	7.54	0.27	1.73	13.54	9.69	2.71	2.35	5.69	6.28	16.05	26.06	6.00
Newry and Mourne	13,556	1.08	8.14	0.17	2.13	19.22	5.85	2.49	3.59	6.17	6.57	16.41	23.19	4.99
Newtownabbey	16,863	0.38	6.74	0.33	1.44	20.54	5.05	5.66	5.79	8.66	7.74	12.54	19.85	5.29
North Down	15,744	0.24	5.60	0.22	1.25	17.22	5.54	3.37	5.39	9.05	11.09	13.06	22.39	5.59
Omagh	7,887	2.03	6.01	0.55	1.67	15.89	5.63	2.10	3.12	6.52	8.29	17.69	25.81	4.69
Strabane	5,565	1.65	17.00	0.29	1.56	17.36	5.70	1.53	2.62	5.10	8.37	14.23	19.91	4.67
Health and Social Services Board														
Eastern	127,920	0.47	5.51	0.28	1.17	17.13	5.67	3.18	4.76	9.19	9.60	13.01	23.97	6.06
Northern	82,491	1.19	9.09	0.29	1.66	18.52	6.57	3.68	3.86	6.81	7.68	13.50	22.49	4.65
Southern	54,034	1.38	10.97	0.21	1.69	18.26	5.66	2.64	3.18	6.54	7.92	14.09	22.95	4.51
Western	44,808	1.28	10.14	0.31	1.55	17.51	6.52	2.53	2.76	6.57	7.88	15.65	22.77	4.52

Area	All females aged 16-74 in employment	Percentage of females aged 16-74 in employment working in:												
		Agriculture, hunting, forestry and fishing	Manufac-turing	Electricity, gas and water supply	Mining & quarrying and construction	Wholesale & retail trade, repair of motor vehicles	Hotels and catering	Transport, storage and communic-ation	Financial intermed-iation	Real estate, renting and business activities	Public adminis-tration and defence	Education	Health and social work	Other[1]
Education and Library Board														
Belfast	**49,022**	0.12	4.76	0.33	0.88	16.92	6.35	3.50	4.50	10.67	8.05	13.70	23.60	6.62
North Eastern	**77,278**	1.14	9.07	0.30	1.63	18.45	6.52	3.80	3.91	6.89	7.73	13.34	22.54	4.66
South Eastern	**78,898**	0.69	5.98	0.24	1.35	17.26	5.24	2.99	4.92	8.27	10.56	12.58	24.21	5.71
Southern	**59,247**	1.43	10.83	0.20	1.73	18.38	5.80	2.58	3.17	6.45	7.83	14.24	22.84	4.51
Western	**44,808**	1.28	10.14	0.31	1.55	17.51	6.52	2.53	2.76	6.57	7.88	15.65	22.77	4.52
Parliamentary Constituency														
Belfast East	**15,528**	0.17	5.51	0.31	1.06	16.43	5.22	3.64	5.20	10.55	10.38	12.59	22.29	6.64
Belfast North	**13,424**	0.09	5.56	0.34	0.82	19.25	6.46	4.63	4.24	9.71	7.31	12.77	22.42	6.42
Belfast South	**21,178**	0.10	4.41	0.36	0.78	14.97	6.49	2.92	4.73	11.62	7.60	15.67	24.16	6.19
Belfast West	**12,022**	0.06	3.93	0.27	0.91	18.97	6.24	3.43	4.34	8.84	7.89	11.71	26.43	6.98
East Antrim	**17,381**	0.66	9.16	0.45	1.27	17.62	6.04	5.71	5.02	7.43	7.76	13.03	20.79	5.07
East Londonderry	**16,079**	1.15	10.05	0.19	1.49	19.43	8.26	1.78	2.43	5.77	8.58	15.78	20.59	4.51
Fermanagh and South Tyrone	**15,490**	2.23	10.29	0.17	1.56	17.28	6.80	2.98	2.79	5.26	6.95	15.38	23.87	4.46
Foyle	**16,280**	0.34	9.34	0.29	1.21	18.62	6.63	2.68	2.57	8.43	7.44	16.03	21.97	4.47
Lagan Valley	**21,677**	0.87	7.81	0.21	1.76	19.11	4.85	2.88	4.51	7.56	10.09	12.16	22.94	5.25
Mid Ulster	**14,069**	1.66	9.32	0.18	2.71	17.32	6.36	1.98	3.28	5.67	7.46	16.20	23.53	4.34
Newry and Armagh	**16,654**	1.56	8.35	0.21	1.55	18.33	5.61	2.40	3.26	6.02	7.73	15.37	25.11	4.49
North Antrim	**19,235**	1.87	10.78	0.33	1.71	19.12	6.59	2.31	2.84	6.25	7.00	13.30	23.59	4.31
North Down	**17,571**	0.36	5.54	0.20	1.26	17.23	5.65	3.36	5.28	8.98	10.95	12.81	22.74	5.65
South Antrim	**21,026**	0.86	7.77	0.24	1.66	17.69	5.78	5.05	4.87	7.85	8.60	11.56	23.51	4.55
South Down	**18,472**	1.46	6.16	0.19	1.92	16.38	6.04	2.48	3.44	6.52	8.66	14.92	26.17	5.65
Strangford	**20,777**	0.98	6.31	0.27	1.37	17.06	4.73	2.96	5.38	8.41	11.34	11.01	24.36	5.82
Upper Bann	**18,938**	0.68	14.48	0.28	1.32	18.92	5.92	2.92	3.10	7.20	8.32	11.96	20.50	4.39
West Tyrone	**13,452**	1.87	10.56	0.44	1.63	16.50	5.66	1.87	2.91	5.93	8.33	16.26	23.37	4.68
NUTS Level III														
Belfast	**49,022**	0.12	4.76	0.33	0.88	16.92	6.35	3.50	4.50	10.67	8.05	13.70	23.60	6.62
Outer Belfast	**76,760**	0.41	6.51	0.26	1.32	18.31	5.08	3.97	5.38	8.51	9.64	12.62	22.53	5.47
East of Northern Ireland	**77,408**	1.25	9.57	0.31	1.56	17.46	6.04	3.15	3.65	7.16	9.04	12.13	23.80	4.88
North of Northern Ireland	**45,296**	1.07	10.87	0.24	1.44	18.49	7.21	2.16	2.53	6.61	7.86	15.32	21.64	4.55
West and South of Northern Ireland	**60,767**	1.79	8.80	0.23	1.93	17.56	6.07	2.45	3.15	5.84	7.43	15.91	24.26	4.56

Note:
1 Other includes: other community, social and personal service activities, private households with employed persons and extra-territorial organisations and bodies.

Table KS12a: Occupation Groups – All Persons

Area	All persons aged 16-74 in employment	Percentage of persons aged 16-74 in employment working in:								
		Managers and senior officials	Professional occupations	Associate professional and technical occupations	Administrative and secretarial occupations	Skilled trades occupations	Personal service occupations	Sales and customer service occupations	Process, plant and machine operatives	Elementary occupations
Northern Ireland	**686,644**	**10.60**	**10.56**	**12.53**	**14.58**	**15.57**	**6.67**	**7.33**	**10.38**	**11.79**
Local Government District										
Antrim	**22,438**	10.75	7.99	16.32	13.24	15.30	6.94	5.91	10.51	13.03
Ards	**33,268**	11.37	8.39	12.43	17.71	16.20	7.37	7.34	8.97	10.23
Armagh	**22,302**	9.79	9.06	11.73	13.41	19.51	7.25	5.74	11.72	11.79
Ballymena	**26,499**	10.63	8.65	10.83	13.47	17.50	5.59	8.16	12.79	12.39
Ballymoney	**11,275**	8.48	6.85	9.74	11.89	22.38	6.30	6.63	15.58	12.15
Banbridge	**18,758**	11.01	8.93	12.39	13.64	18.72	6.69	6.10	12.26	10.27
Belfast	**100,826**	9.85	14.39	12.54	16.19	9.64	6.48	9.32	7.27	14.33
Carrickfergus	**17,176**	11.10	9.00	13.21	17.64	13.09	6.65	7.24	10.33	11.74
Castlereagh	**30,244**	12.70	14.11	14.90	18.25	10.12	6.49	7.08	6.86	9.49
Coleraine	**23,156**	10.82	11.51	11.69	13.50	14.77	6.51	8.62	10.09	12.50
Cookstown	**12,382**	9.56	8.70	8.90	10.69	24.29	6.16	5.97	12.36	13.36
Craigavon	**32,993**	9.83	8.36	11.68	13.75	14.63	6.10	7.06	16.65	11.93
Derry	**36,225**	10.01	11.88	14.07	13.10	12.70	6.69	7.98	11.53	12.04
Down	**26,881**	11.06	9.86	12.97	14.62	18.71	8.55	5.35	8.54	10.35
Dungannon	**18,461**	9.50	9.87	9.98	11.80	21.80	6.54	5.19	13.34	11.98
Fermanagh	**22,782**	9.21	9.45	10.09	11.38	21.63	7.11	7.05	11.78	12.30
Larne	**13,467**	10.02	7.89	11.15	14.26	17.30	6.30	7.01	13.94	12.13
Limavady	**12,945**	7.74	7.70	14.03	13.13	18.36	6.27	5.08	14.65	13.04
Lisburn	**47,400**	12.69	10.73	14.85	15.70	12.84	6.46	8.03	8.72	9.98
Magherafelt	**16,477**	8.66	9.50	9.95	11.37	25.28	5.75	5.60	12.60	11.28
Moyle	**5,949**	9.09	9.85	9.75	10.52	24.76	8.37	5.16	10.25	12.24
Newry and Mourne	**31,873**	9.73	10.14	9.74	11.87	21.82	6.93	6.83	11.03	11.89
Newtownabbey	**36,291**	11.66	10.04	12.41	17.28	12.70	6.01	8.92	9.29	11.69
North Down	**34,629**	14.65	12.52	16.34	17.25	9.80	7.01	7.50	6.13	8.79
Omagh	**18,606**	9.15	10.40	13.16	12.22	21.44	7.22	5.58	9.96	10.86
Strabane	**13,341**	7.86	7.28	8.99	11.99	21.07	6.79	6.26	17.04	12.72
Health and Social Services Board										
Eastern	**273,248**	11.57	12.31	13.71	16.50	11.96	6.85	7.98	7.66	11.45
Northern	**185,110**	10.44	9.18	11.85	14.07	17.20	6.29	7.36	11.39	12.21
Southern	**124,387**	9.93	9.25	11.05	12.90	19.03	6.67	6.34	13.17	11.65
Western	**103,899**	9.12	9.97	12.38	12.43	18.00	6.84	6.76	12.40	12.10

Area	All persons aged 16-74 in employment	Percentage of persons aged 16-74 in employment working in:								
		Managers and senior officials	Professional occupations	Associate professional and technical occupations	Administrative and secretarial occupations	Skilled trades occupations	Personal service occupations	Sales and customer service occupations	Process, plant and machine operatives	Elementary occupations
Education and Library Board										
Belfast	100,826	9.85	14.39	12.54	16.19	9.64	6.48	9.32	7.27	14.33
North Eastern	172,728	10.50	9.22	12.06	14.32	16.70	6.29	7.46	11.32	12.13
South Eastern	172,422	12.58	11.09	14.40	16.68	13.32	7.08	7.20	7.89	9.76
Southern	136,769	9.89	9.20	10.85	12.70	19.51	6.63	6.31	13.10	11.81
Western	103,899	9.12	9.97	12.38	12.43	18.00	6.84	6.76	12.40	12.10
Parliamentary Constituency										
Belfast East	32,555	11.80	13.01	13.69	18.03	9.96	6.36	8.20	7.21	11.74
Belfast North	27,898	8.26	8.87	10.09	15.71	12.00	7.48	9.70	9.96	17.93
Belfast South	42,633	11.84	22.69	15.38	14.90	6.58	5.26	8.72	4.52	10.11
Belfast West	24,946	6.71	6.15	9.43	17.72	12.88	7.96	10.85	10.11	18.18
East Antrim	37,785	11.13	9.71	12.45	16.10	14.20	6.24	7.29	11.17	11.71
East Londonderry	36,101	9.71	10.14	12.53	13.37	16.05	6.42	7.35	11.72	12.69
Fermanagh and South Tyrone	36,315	9.37	9.61	10.14	11.43	21.37	6.93	6.27	12.51	12.38
Foyle	36,225	10.01	11.88	14.07	13.10	12.70	6.69	7.98	11.53	12.04
Lagan Valley	47,659	13.20	11.00	15.34	15.43	13.28	6.33	7.35	8.66	9.42
Mid Ulster	33,787	9.06	9.26	9.47	11.30	24.75	5.98	5.77	12.47	11.94
Newry and Armagh	38,146	9.67	9.48	11.04	12.87	19.18	7.28	6.55	11.40	12.52
North Antrim	43,723	9.86	8.35	10.40	12.66	19.74	6.15	7.36	13.16	12.30
North Down	38,677	14.41	12.14	15.88	17.11	10.43	7.22	7.43	6.38	9.01
South Antrim	47,022	11.38	8.80	14.48	15.87	14.06	6.41	7.46	9.83	11.73
South Down	43,035	10.29	9.73	11.38	13.15	21.96	7.72	5.74	9.72	10.31
Strangford	45,358	11.72	9.38	13.03	17.94	15.12	7.15	6.89	8.75	10.02
Upper Bann	42,832	10.24	8.52	12.00	13.76	14.87	6.20	6.94	15.73	11.74
West Tyrone	31,947	8.61	9.10	11.42	12.12	21.29	7.04	5.87	12.92	11.63
NUTS Level III										
Belfast	100,826	9.85	14.39	12.54	16.19	9.64	6.48	9.32	7.27	14.33
Outer Belfast	165,740	12.71	11.39	14.47	17.04	11.70	6.50	7.86	8.13	10.20
East of Northern Ireland	174,304	10.69	8.62	12.53	14.56	16.73	6.83	6.76	11.87	11.41
North of Northern Ireland	102,891	9.41	10.00	12.15	12.77	16.72	6.66	7.22	12.68	12.38
West and South of Northern Ireland	142,883	9.41	9.66	10.53	11.91	21.99	6.79	6.11	11.71	11.87

KS12b

Table KS12b: Occupation Groups – Males

Area	All males aged 16-74 in employment	Percentage of males aged 16-74 in employment working in:								
		Managers and senior officials	Professional occupations	Associate professional and technical occupations	Administrative and secretarial occupations	Skilled trades occupations	Personal service occupations	Sales and customer service occupations	Process, plant and machine operatives	Elementary occupations
Northern Ireland	**377,391**	**12.64**	**10.11**	**11.79**	**7.17**	**25.68**	**1.75**	**3.73**	**15.50**	**11.64**
Local Government District										
Antrim	12,715	13.02	7.41	17.48	6.33	24.35	1.77	2.61	14.90	12.14
Ards	18,138	13.51	8.44	11.97	9.55	27.46	1.47	3.45	13.85	10.30
Armagh	12,537	11.25	7.82	10.03	5.97	31.28	1.80	3.01	17.85	10.99
Ballymena	14,636	13.21	7.80	9.65	5.58	28.48	1.21	3.81	18.37	11.90
Ballymoney	6,451	9.49	5.80	8.01	4.19	35.85	1.58	3.33	20.40	11.35
Banbridge	10,579	12.66	8.25	10.80	6.63	30.00	1.19	2.73	17.60	10.13
Belfast	51,804	12.03	15.39	11.69	9.39	16.71	2.29	5.34	12.27	14.89
Carrickfergus	9,180	13.46	9.69	13.91	9.37	22.11	1.73	3.17	15.20	11.35
Castlereagh	15,767	15.76	15.11	13.59	10.26	17.85	1.72	4.17	11.48	10.07
Coleraine	12,472	12.87	10.76	11.92	7.27	24.21	2.04	4.20	14.87	11.87
Cookstown	7,169	10.74	6.47	6.96	3.91	38.18	1.16	2.36	18.06	12.16
Craigavon	18,378	11.73	7.82	10.72	6.26	23.82	1.47	3.32	22.54	12.31
Derry	19,945	12.17	11.23	14.76	6.17	20.58	2.53	4.37	16.51	11.68
Down	15,014	12.93	9.20	12.38	6.75	30.62	2.02	2.77	13.29	10.03
Dungannon	10,542	11.00	7.80	7.07	4.53	35.00	1.38	2.66	19.06	11.50
Fermanagh	13,101	10.07	7.95	8.34	5.56	33.60	1.86	3.41	17.24	11.98
Larne	7,436	11.44	7.60	9.92	6.59	28.17	1.49	3.13	19.80	11.85
Limavady	7,550	8.62	6.44	15.47	6.24	29.30	1.38	2.15	18.34	12.07
Lisburn	25,720	15.44	11.10	14.78	8.00	21.29	1.40	4.07	13.76	10.15
Magherafelt	9,731	9.64	7.48	6.66	3.70	39.64	1.10	2.95	18.13	10.71
Moyle	3,401	9.44	7.85	8.06	4.26	38.99	2.12	2.50	14.44	12.35
Newry and Mourne	18,317	11.16	8.37	7.48	4.48	35.05	1.83	3.26	16.94	11.43
Newtownabbey	19,428	14.50	10.39	12.39	8.31	21.44	1.59	4.53	14.73	12.11
North Down	18,885	18.56	13.34	17.77	10.15	16.28	1.62	4.24	9.57	8.47
Omagh	10,719	10.93	8.29	12.05	5.48	33.93	1.99	2.81	14.54	9.97
Strabane	7,776	8.76	6.11	8.11	5.09	33.08	1.89	3.14	20.54	13.28
Health and Social Services Board										
Eastern	145,328	14.17	12.83	13.34	9.09	20.36	1.85	4.34	12.40	11.62
Northern	102,619	12.41	8.51	11.19	6.38	28.07	1.56	3.48	16.60	11.80
Southern	70,353	11.53	8.03	9.22	5.54	30.68	1.57	3.06	18.98	11.40
Western	59,091	10.58	8.68	12.06	5.78	28.65	2.05	3.43	17.08	11.70

© Crown copyright 2002

42

Area	All males aged 16-74 in employment	Percentage of males aged 16-74 in employment working in:								
		Managers and senior officials	Professional occupations	Associate professional and technical occupations	Administrative and secretarial occupations	Skilled trades occupations	Personal service occupations	Sales and customer service occupations	Process, plant and machine operatives	Elementary occupations
Education and Library Board										
Belfast	51,804	12.03	15.39	11.69	9.39	16.71	2.29	5.34	12.27	14.89
North Eastern	95,450	12.54	8.66	11.51	6.57	27.31	1.59	3.57	16.49	11.77
South Eastern	93,524	15.35	11.41	14.25	8.92	22.39	1.61	3.79	12.47	9.81
Southern	77,522	11.45	7.88	9.01	5.39	31.37	1.53	3.00	18.90	11.47
Western	59,091	10.58	8.68	12.06	5.78	28.65	2.05	3.43	17.08	11.70
Parliamentary Constituency										
Belfast East	17,027	14.45	13.90	13.56	10.05	17.27	1.94	4.49	11.93	12.42
Belfast North	14,474	10.04	9.20	9.67	8.35	20.39	2.75	4.91	16.35	18.34
Belfast South	21,455	14.84	24.88	13.29	9.64	11.53	1.89	5.73	7.70	10.50
Belfast West	12,924	7.84	6.48	8.96	9.38	22.50	2.65	5.97	17.54	18.69
East Antrim	20,404	13.27	10.03	12.36	8.06	23.67	1.59	3.31	16.29	11.42
East Londonderry	20,022	11.27	9.13	13.26	6.88	26.13	1.79	3.43	16.18	11.94
Fermanagh and South Tyrone	20,825	10.46	7.98	8.04	5.19	33.45	1.69	3.08	17.98	12.14
Foyle	19,945	12.17	11.23	14.76	6.17	20.58	2.53	4.37	16.51	11.68
Lagan Valley	25,982	15.96	11.35	15.08	7.76	21.95	1.26	3.64	13.34	9.65
Mid Ulster	19,718	10.18	7.07	6.65	3.88	39.16	1.16	2.75	18.16	10.99
Newry and Armagh	21,492	10.94	8.09	9.10	5.67	30.96	2.12	3.48	17.70	11.94
North Antrim	24,488	11.70	7.28	9.00	5.03	31.89	1.43	3.50	18.36	11.81
North Down	21,106	18.17	12.92	17.14	9.99	17.33	1.64	4.11	9.97	8.75
South Antrim	25,996	14.00	8.53	15.04	7.57	23.04	1.63	3.62	14.85	11.72
South Down	24,563	11.92	8.39	9.96	5.33	35.35	1.65	2.65	14.86	9.90
Strangford	24,581	14.09	9.60	12.35	9.61	25.80	1.40	3.47	13.55	10.13
Upper Bann	23,894	12.20	8.01	11.09	6.56	24.04	1.46	3.21	21.48	11.95
West Tyrone	18,495	10.02	7.37	10.40	5.31	33.57	1.95	2.95	17.06	11.37
NUTS Level III										
Belfast	51,804	12.03	15.39	11.69	9.39	16.71	2.29	5.34	12.27	14.89
Outer Belfast	88,980	15.75	11.99	14.59	9.07	19.73	1.58	4.13	12.83	10.33
East of Northern Ireland	96,896	12.72	8.12	11.88	6.92	27.34	1.53	3.16	17.10	11.22
North of Northern Ireland	57,595	10.93	9.00	12.19	5.94	26.99	2.06	3.65	17.25	11.99
West and South of Northern Ireland	82,116	10.73	7.87	8.41	4.87	34.91	1.65	2.99	17.32	11.25

KS12b

Table KS12c: Occupation Groups – Females

Area	All females aged 16-74 in employment	Percentage of females aged 16-74 in employment working in:								
		Managers and senior officials	Professional occupations	Associate professional and technical occupations	Administrative and secretarial occupations	Skilled trades occupations	Personal service occupations	Sales and customer service occupations	Process, plant and machine operatives	Elementary occupations
Northern Ireland	**309,253**	**8.11**	**11.11**	**13.43**	**23.62**	**3.23**	**12.66**	**11.73**	**4.14**	**11.97**
Local Government District										
Antrim	9,723	7.80	8.75	14.82	22.27	3.47	13.70	10.23	4.76	14.20
Ards	15,130	8.80	8.33	12.97	27.48	2.72	14.45	12.00	3.11	10.13
Armagh	9,765	7.92	10.64	13.93	22.97	4.40	14.23	9.25	3.85	12.81
Ballymena	11,863	7.44	9.69	12.29	23.22	3.95	10.98	13.54	5.91	12.99
Ballymoney	4,824	7.13	8.25	12.04	22.20	4.35	12.60	11.05	9.14	13.23
Banbridge	8,179	8.88	9.81	14.44	22.70	4.13	13.80	10.45	5.34	10.44
Belfast	49,022	7.55	13.34	13.44	23.38	2.16	10.90	13.52	1.99	13.73
Carrickfergus	7,996	8.38	8.20	12.41	27.13	2.74	12.31	11.91	4.74	12.19
Castlereagh	14,477	9.37	13.03	16.32	26.97	1.70	11.68	10.25	1.82	8.86
Coleraine	10,684	8.42	12.38	11.43	20.78	3.74	11.73	13.77	4.51	13.23
Cookstown	5,213	7.94	11.76	11.57	20.03	5.20	13.04	10.93	4.53	15.00
Craigavon	14,615	7.44	9.04	12.88	23.17	3.09	11.93	11.76	9.24	11.45
Derry	16,280	7.36	12.68	13.22	21.59	3.05	11.78	12.39	5.44	12.48
Down	11,867	8.69	10.69	13.73	24.57	3.64	16.79	8.61	2.53	10.75
Dungannon	7,919	7.50	12.64	13.85	21.47	4.22	13.40	8.56	5.73	12.63
Fermanagh	9,681	8.05	11.50	12.45	19.25	5.42	14.21	11.98	4.40	12.74
Larne	6,031	8.27	8.24	12.65	23.73	3.90	12.24	11.79	6.72	12.47
Limavady	5,395	6.51	9.47	12.01	22.78	3.06	13.12	9.18	9.47	14.40
Lisburn	21,680	9.43	10.29	14.94	24.83	2.82	12.46	12.72	2.74	9.77
Magherafelt	6,746	7.25	12.41	14.69	22.44	4.58	12.47	9.43	4.62	12.11
Moyle	2,548	8.63	12.52	12.01	18.88	5.77	16.72	8.71	4.67	12.09
Newry and Mourne	13,556	7.80	12.53	12.80	21.86	3.95	13.83	11.66	3.06	12.52
Newtownabbey	16,863	8.38	9.64	12.44	27.61	2.63	11.11	13.98	3.02	11.21
North Down	15,744	9.96	11.54	14.63	25.77	2.03	13.48	11.41	2.00	9.18
Omagh	7,887	6.73	13.26	14.67	21.39	4.48	14.33	9.36	3.73	12.06
Strabane	5,565	6.61	8.91	10.22	21.62	4.29	13.64	10.62	12.15	11.93
Health and Social Services Board										
Eastern	127,920	8.62	11.73	14.14	24.92	2.41	12.54	12.12	2.28	11.25
Northern	82,491	7.99	10.02	12.67	23.65	3.68	12.17	12.19	4.91	12.73
Southern	54,034	7.84	10.85	13.43	22.49	3.86	13.32	10.61	5.61	11.98
Western	44,808	7.20	11.67	12.79	21.20	3.97	13.15	11.16	6.23	12.62

Area	All females aged 16-74 in employment	Percentage of females aged 16-74 in employment working in:								
		Managers and senior officials	Professional occupations	Associate professional and technical occupations	Administrative and secretarial occupations	Skilled trades occupations	Personal service occupations	Sales and customer service occupations	Process, plant and machine operatives	Elementary occupations
Education and Library Board										
Belfast	49,022	7.55	13.34	13.44	23.38	2.16	10.90	13.52	1.99	13.73
North Eastern	77,278	7.99	9.91	12.75	23.89	3.58	12.11	12.27	4.93	12.57
South Eastern	78,898	9.29	10.73	14.57	25.88	2.56	13.55	11.25	2.46	9.70
Southern	59,247	7.85	10.93	13.26	22.27	3.98	13.30	10.64	5.32	12.25
Western	44,808	7.20	11.67	12.79	21.20	3.97	13.15	11.16	6.23	12.62
Parliamentary Constituency										
Belfast East	15,528	8.91	12.04	13.84	26.77	1.94	11.22	12.26	2.03	10.99
Belfast North	13,424	6.34	8.51	10.56	23.64	2.96	12.59	14.85	3.08	17.48
Belfast South	21,178	8.80	20.47	17.51	20.23	1.57	8.66	11.74	1.29	9.72
Belfast West	12,022	5.51	5.80	9.94	26.69	2.54	13.67	16.09	2.13	17.64
East Antrim	17,381	8.62	9.34	12.57	25.54	3.08	11.69	11.96	5.16	12.04
East Londonderry	16,079	7.78	11.41	11.62	21.45	3.51	12.20	12.23	6.18	13.63
Fermanagh and South Tyrone	15,490	7.90	11.80	12.96	19.82	5.15	13.97	10.57	5.15	12.69
Foyle	16,280	7.36	12.68	13.22	21.59	3.05	11.78	12.39	5.44	12.48
Lagan Valley	21,677	9.88	10.58	15.65	24.63	2.87	12.40	11.80	3.05	9.14
Mid Ulster	14,069	7.48	12.34	13.43	21.69	4.56	12.75	10.00	4.49	13.26
Newry and Armagh	16,654	8.03	11.29	13.55	22.16	3.99	13.93	10.52	3.26	13.26
North Antrim	19,235	7.52	9.70	12.19	22.39	4.29	12.15	12.27	6.56	12.93
North Down	17,571	9.90	11.22	14.36	25.67	2.14	13.91	11.41	2.06	9.33
South Antrim	21,026	8.15	9.13	13.77	26.13	2.96	12.31	12.20	3.61	11.74
South Down	18,472	8.13	11.53	13.27	23.57	4.15	15.79	9.85	2.88	10.85
Strangford	20,777	8.91	9.12	13.83	27.80	2.50	13.94	10.94	3.07	9.90
Upper Bann	18,938	7.76	9.17	13.15	22.85	3.29	12.19	11.63	8.48	11.48
West Tyrone	13,452	6.68	11.46	12.83	21.48	4.40	14.04	9.88	7.21	12.01
NUTS Level III										
Belfast	49,022	7.55	13.34	13.44	23.38	2.16	10.90	13.52	1.99	13.73
Outer Belfast	76,760	9.19	10.70	14.32	26.28	2.40	12.21	12.18	2.68	10.04
East of Northern Ireland	77,408	8.16	9.23	13.33	24.12	3.45	13.47	11.27	5.33	11.64
North of Northern Ireland	45,296	7.47	11.28	12.09	21.46	3.66	12.52	11.76	6.87	12.88
West and South of Northern Ireland	60,767	7.63	12.09	13.41	21.42	4.54	13.75	10.31	4.14	12.72

Table KS13: Qualifications and Students

Area	All persons aged 16-74	Percentage of persons aged 16-74 with:						Total number of full-time students and schoolchildren[6]		Percentage of full-time students aged 18-74:		
		No qualifications	Highest qualification attained: Level 1[1]	Highest qualification attained: Level 2[2]	Highest qualification attained: Level 3[3]	Highest qualification attained: Level 4[4]	Highest qualification attained: Level 5[5]	Aged 16-17	Aged 18-74	Economically active — In employment	Economically active — Unemployed	Economically inactive
Northern Ireland	**1,187,079**	**41.64**	**17.23**	**16.36**	**8.98**	**10.93**	**4.87**	**43,286**	**50,503**	**33.89**	**3.74**	**62.36**
Local Government District												
Antrim	34,579	38.73	20.04	17.95	8.91	10.43	3.94	1,052	1,039	37.54	2.50	59.96
Ards	52,878	39.30	19.90	17.46	8.86	10.39	4.09	1,667	1,501	36.64	3.80	59.56
Armagh	37,752	43.64	17.04	16.65	9.06	9.73	3.88	1,649	1,274	27.39	3.22	69.39
Ballymena	41,948	45.00	15.80	17.11	8.08	10.55	3.46	1,379	1,152	35.59	2.43	61.98
Ballymoney	18,887	48.74	18.01	16.43	6.72	7.39	2.72	709	481	29.11	3.12	67.78
Banbridge	29,283	41.68	17.93	17.41	8.62	10.52	3.85	1,017	874	32.49	2.52	64.99
Belfast	197,519	41.82	14.76	13.31	10.88	12.24	6.97	6,366	15,483	35.15	4.00	60.85
Carrickfergus	26,951	37.96	19.53	17.63	9.20	11.42	4.26	835	882	43.76	3.06	53.17
Castlereagh	47,155	35.52	16.77	16.53	9.02	14.76	7.40	1,311	1,490	43.02	2.95	54.03
Coleraine	40,089	39.85	16.40	16.37	10.07	11.60	5.71	1,366	2,932	35.10	3.89	61.02
Cookstown	22,417	47.86	16.63	16.67	7.74	7.81	3.29	1,002	767	29.86	2.48	67.67
Craigavon	56,305	45.61	17.13	16.46	7.97	9.31	3.51	2,120	1,573	36.24	3.05	60.71
Derry	72,665	43.69	17.19	15.55	8.47	10.23	4.86	3,211	3,392	30.13	5.51	64.36
Down	44,249	38.19	18.14	18.33	9.33	11.29	4.73	1,765	1,549	30.66	3.94	65.40
Dungannon	32,835	44.94	16.25	17.12	7.96	9.98	3.76	1,393	1,105	26.24	3.62	70.14
Fermanagh	39,898	44.79	17.84	16.79	7.07	9.54	3.98	1,759	1,252	24.04	4.15	71.81
Larne	22,086	41.92	18.96	17.35	8.08	9.87	3.82	717	524	35.88	3.63	60.50
Limavady	22,761	46.92	18.00	16.45	8.22	7.43	2.97	829	711	25.18	4.50	70.32
Lisburn	76,476	37.39	18.45	17.58	9.01	12.20	5.37	2,763	2,749	39.69	4.00	56.31
Magherafelt	27,424	44.33	17.11	16.96	8.23	9.51	3.85	1,123	909	22.99	2.64	74.37
Moyle	11,073	44.82	17.18	17.66	7.03	9.52	3.79	458	331	22.36	3.93	73.72
Newry and Mourne	59,568	44.06	17.21	16.46	8.60	9.44	4.23	2,513	2,007	26.06	3.69	70.25
Newtownabbey	57,907	39.03	18.50	16.56	9.59	11.57	4.75	1,789	2,618	41.21	3.21	55.58
North Down	54,882	30.98	18.13	19.57	9.94	15.09	6.29	1,914	2,057	38.75	3.21	58.05
Omagh	33,045	43.34	17.93	16.74	7.56	10.48	3.95	1,547	1,061	26.39	2.83	70.78
Strabane	26,447	53.96	15.98	14.07	6.70	6.64	2.64	1,032	790	23.80	4.94	71.27
Health and Social Services Board												
Eastern	473,159	38.60	16.84	15.98	9.91	12.52	6.15	15,786	24,829	36.24	3.85	59.91
Northern	303,361	41.99	17.81	17.00	8.69	10.37	4.15	10,430	11,635	35.53	3.17	61.30
Southern	215,743	44.20	17.11	16.72	8.42	9.69	3.86	8,692	6,833	29.50	3.29	67.20
Western	194,816	45.63	17.38	15.91	7.76	9.32	4.00	8,378	7,206	27.34	4.72	67.94

Table KS13: Qualifications and Students (continued)

Area	All persons aged 16-74	Percentage of persons aged 16-74 with:						Total number of full-time students and schoolchildren[6]		Percentage of full-time students aged 18-74:		
		No qualifications	Highest qualification attained: Level 1[1]	Highest qualification attained: Level 2[2]	Highest qualification attained: Level 3[3]	Highest qualification attained: Level 4[4]	Highest qualification attained: Level 5[5]	Aged 16-17	Aged 18-74	Economically active: In employment	Economically active: Unemployed	Economically inactive
Education and Library Board												
Belfast	197,519	41.82	14.76	13.31	10.88	12.24	6.97	6,366	15,483	35.15	4.00	60.85
North Eastern	280,944	41.52	17.90	17.02	8.77	10.57	4.21	9,428	10,868	35.93	3.22	60.85
South Eastern	275,640	36.29	18.33	17.90	9.22	12.72	5.55	9,420	9,346	38.03	3.62	58.36
Southern	238,160	44.55	17.06	16.72	8.36	9.51	3.81	9,694	7,600	29.54	3.21	67.25
Western	194,816	45.63	17.38	15.91	7.76	9.32	4.00	8,378	7,206	27.34	4.72	67.94
Parliamentary Constituency												
Belfast East	55,969	40.68	16.26	15.41	8.13	13.29	6.22	1,579	1,638	38.10	3.54	58.36
Belfast North	59,503	51.40	17.19	13.23	6.88	7.53	3.77	2,086	1,937	36.96	4.23	58.80
Belfast South	71,904	26.52	10.47	12.41	17.18	20.41	13.01	1,676	11,113	34.90	3.76	61.34
Belfast West	58,818	51.46	18.42	14.05	7.72	5.66	2.68	2,686	2,538	34.63	5.44	59.93
East Antrim	60,400	38.31	18.78	17.17	9.43	11.50	4.81	1,862	2,506	38.51	3.35	58.14
East Londonderry	62,850	42.41	16.98	16.40	9.40	10.09	4.72	2,195	3,643	33.16	4.01	62.83
Fermanagh and South Tyrone	63,234	44.87	17.10	16.92	7.37	9.80	3.93	2,724	1,975	25.22	3.85	70.94
Foyle	72,665	43.69	17.19	15.55	8.47	10.23	4.86	3,211	3,392	30.13	5.51	64.36
Lagan Valley	72,778	36.17	18.13	17.79	9.13	13.05	5.73	2,298	2,329	40.92	3.31	55.78
Mid Ulster	59,340	45.73	16.95	16.87	8.02	8.84	3.59	2,553	2,058	25.80	2.87	71.33
Newry and Armagh	69,832	44.66	17.01	16.41	8.67	9.30	3.95	3,018	2,382	26.95	3.27	69.77
North Antrim	71,908	45.95	16.59	17.01	7.56	9.56	3.32	2,546	1,964	31.77	2.85	65.38
North Down	61,680	32.14	18.18	19.35	9.76	14.51	6.06	2,135	2,210	38.19	3.17	58.64
South Antrim	71,898	38.04	19.54	17.95	9.17	11.19	4.12	2,291	2,277	42.73	2.81	54.46
South Down	72,072	40.40	17.73	17.72	9.18	10.56	4.41	2,925	2,448	28.43	3.88	67.69
Strangford	70,645	37.90	19.47	17.53	9.05	11.35	4.69	2,227	2,157	40.15	3.29	56.56
Upper Bann	72,091	44.83	17.27	16.65	8.05	9.62	3.58	2,695	2,085	35.01	3.02	61.97
West Tyrone	59,492	48.06	17.07	15.55	7.17	8.78	3.37	2,579	1,851	25.28	3.73	70.99
NUTS Level III												
Belfast	197,519	41.82	14.76	13.31	10.88	12.24	6.97	6,366	15,483	35.15	4.00	60.85
Outer Belfast	263,371	36.14	18.21	17.59	9.35	13.04	5.68	8,612	9,796	40.77	3.38	55.85
East of Northern Ireland	281,328	41.62	18.19	17.39	8.56	10.32	3.92	9,717	8,212	34.91	3.18	61.91
North of Northern Ireland	191,922	45.25	17.04	15.84	8.27	9.37	4.23	7,605	8,637	30.47	4.63	64.90
West and South of Northern Ireland	252,939	44.50	17.19	16.73	8.09	9.57	3.92	10,986	8,375	26.04	3.34	70.61

Notes:
1 GCSE (grades D-G), CSE (grades 2-5), 1-4 CSEs (grade 1), 1-4 GCSEs (grades A-C), 1-4 'O' level passes, NVQ level 1, GNVQ Foundation or equivalents.
2 5+ CSEs (grade 1), 5+ GCSEs (grades A-C), 5+ 'O' level passes, Senior Certificate, 1 'A' level, 1-3 AS levels, Advanced Senior Certificate, NVQ level 2, GNVQ Intermediate or equivalents.
3 2+ 'A' levels, 4+ AS levels, NVQ level 3, GNVQ Advanced or equivalents.
4 First degree, NVQ level 4, HNC, HND or equivalents.
5 Higher degree, NVQ level 5 or equivalents.
6 All students and schoolchildren are counted at their term-time address.

Table KS14a: National Statistics – Socio Economic Classification – All Persons

Area	All persons aged 16-74	Percentage of persons aged 16-74:										
		Large employers and higher managerial occupations	Higher professional occupations	Lower managerial and professional occupations	Intermediate occupations	Small employers and own account workers	Lower supervisory and technical occupations	Semi-routine occupations	Routine occupations	Never worked	Long-term unemployed[1]	Full-time students[2]
Northern Ireland	**1,187,079**	**2.11**	**3.78**	**19.34**	**11.09**	**8.73**	**8.77**	**15.43**	**16.27**	**4.90**	**1.67**	**7.90**
Local Government District												
Antrim	34,579	2.76	3.28	21.22	12.85	8.86	9.99	14.66	15.10	4.19	1.04	6.05
Ards	52,878	2.44	3.77	20.45	13.63	10.36	9.66	15.75	14.01	2.72	1.21	5.99
Armagh	37,752	1.95	2.79	18.68	10.64	11.95	8.08	13.29	17.83	5.39	1.65	7.74
Ballymena	41,948	2.25	3.04	19.27	10.58	9.95	10.00	18.25	16.18	3.33	1.12	6.03
Ballymoney	18,887	1.42	2.51	15.64	8.88	13.08	8.77	17.44	20.03	4.57	1.36	6.30
Banbridge	29,283	2.18	3.56	19.64	11.12	12.00	9.12	14.59	16.97	3.30	1.07	6.46
Belfast	197,519	1.75	5.40	17.97	10.77	4.06	7.86	15.94	16.66	6.21	2.31	11.06
Carrickfergus	26,951	2.27	3.82	21.41	14.57	5.74	11.09	16.38	14.52	2.61	1.21	6.37
Castlereagh	47,155	3.23	6.39	25.93	15.14	5.93	8.35	14.84	11.21	2.17	0.85	5.94
Coleraine	40,089	1.80	3.90	19.33	10.75	9.80	8.06	15.90	13.73	4.29	1.71	10.72
Cookstown	22,417	1.49	2.30	15.47	7.87	13.83	8.29	14.71	20.16	6.63	1.35	7.89
Craigavon	56,305	2.07	2.70	17.87	10.28	7.70	10.60	18.51	18.29	3.98	1.44	6.56
Derry	72,665	1.88	2.97	18.18	9.11	5.93	8.90	15.23	19.01	6.62	3.08	9.09
Down	44,249	2.11	3.51	21.04	11.29	12.49	8.49	13.62	14.43	4.26	1.29	7.49
Dungannon	32,835	1.75	2.73	16.62	8.77	12.87	7.89	14.79	19.15	6.47	1.36	7.61
Fermanagh	39,898	1.51	2.87	16.26	9.30	12.98	7.94	15.27	17.69	6.61	2.02	7.55
Larne	22,086	1.90	2.96	18.92	11.22	8.74	12.14	17.25	16.33	3.50	1.43	5.62
Limavady	22,761	1.77	2.01	16.32	10.21	9.98	9.14	15.13	20.05	6.55	2.07	6.77
Lisburn	76,476	2.99	4.38	22.52	12.94	7.59	8.45	15.34	13.59	3.76	1.22	7.21
Magherafelt	27,424	1.59	2.65	16.84	8.40	14.32	8.52	14.02	19.76	5.23	1.26	7.41
Moyle	11,073	1.31	2.75	17.65	8.19	14.57	8.08	15.02	16.76	6.41	2.13	7.13
Newry and Mourne	59,568	1.44	2.66	16.79	8.14	12.36	7.96	14.43	19.07	7.48	2.09	7.59
Newtownabbey	57,907	2.57	4.05	21.26	14.17	5.96	10.25	16.14	14.22	2.68	1.08	7.61
North Down	54,882	3.83	5.58	26.61	14.89	7.18	8.21	14.01	9.05	2.35	1.05	7.24
Omagh	33,045	1.45	2.87	19.06	9.28	12.87	7.51	13.64	16.16	7.37	1.91	7.89
Strabane	26,447	1.16	1.72	13.16	7.68	10.96	8.82	14.47	24.83	7.84	2.46	6.89
Health and Social Services Board												
Eastern	473,159	2.45	5.00	21.06	12.40	6.67	8.31	15.27	14.23	4.39	1.62	8.58
Northern	303,361	2.09	3.30	19.26	11.36	9.63	9.64	16.08	16.10	3.98	1.29	7.27
Southern	215,743	1.84	2.83	17.77	9.64	11.10	8.82	15.37	18.38	5.48	1.59	7.20
Western	194,816	1.62	2.65	17.04	9.11	9.71	8.48	14.85	19.17	6.90	2.46	8.00

Table KS14a: National Statistics – Socio Economic Classification – All Persons (continued)

Area	All persons aged 16-74	Percentage of persons aged 16-74:										
		Large employers and higher managerial occupations	Higher professional occupations	Lower managerial and professional occupations	Intermediate occupations	Small employers and own account workers	Lower supervisory and technical occupations	Semi-routine occupations	Routine occupations	Never worked	Long-term unemployed[1]	Full-time students[2]
Education and Library Board												
Belfast	197,519	1.75	5.40	17.97	10.77	4.06	7.86	15.94	16.66	6.21	2.31	11.06
North Eastern	280,944	2.13	3.38	19.56	11.64	9.29	9.74	16.18	15.78	3.77	1.29	7.22
South Eastern	275,640	2.95	4.71	23.28	13.57	8.54	8.62	14.79	12.49	3.09	1.13	6.81
Southern	238,160	1.81	2.78	17.55	9.47	11.36	8.77	15.31	18.54	5.59	1.57	7.26
Western	194,816	1.62	2.65	17.04	9.11	9.71	8.48	14.85	19.17	6.90	2.46	8.00
Parliamentary Constituency												
Belfast East	55,969	2.57	5.57	22.77	13.90	4.74	8.87	16.64	14.18	3.61	1.41	5.75
Belfast North	59,503	1.24	2.81	14.83	10.40	4.11	9.41	19.33	21.34	7.07	2.71	6.76
Belfast South	71,904	2.67	10.15	23.37	10.75	4.20	5.84	11.02	9.66	3.35	1.20	17.79
Belfast West	58,818	0.88	1.62	12.28	10.31	3.78	8.47	18.71	21.50	9.92	3.65	8.88
East Antrim	60,400	2.35	4.00	20.73	12.99	6.70	11.02	16.26	14.69	2.82	1.22	7.23
East Londonderry	62,850	1.79	3.22	18.24	10.56	9.86	8.46	15.62	16.02	5.10	1.84	9.29
Fermanagh and South Tyrone	63,234	1.63	2.90	16.49	9.16	13.07	7.86	15.23	18.05	6.44	1.74	7.43
Foyle	72,665	1.88	2.97	18.18	9.11	5.93	8.90	15.23	19.01	6.62	3.08	9.09
Lagan Valley	72,778	3.27	4.79	24.06	13.33	8.59	8.60	14.61	12.99	2.62	0.78	6.36
Mid Ulster	59,340	1.55	2.44	16.18	8.20	13.77	8.40	14.26	20.01	6.08	1.35	7.77
Newry and Armagh	69,832	1.61	2.57	17.42	9.36	10.99	8.06	13.85	19.11	7.23	2.07	7.73
North Antrim	71,908	1.89	2.86	18.07	9.77	11.49	9.38	17.54	17.28	4.13	1.34	6.27
North Down	61,680	3.70	5.40	25.98	14.64	7.52	8.41	14.31	9.52	2.38	1.08	7.04
South Antrim	71,898	2.71	3.56	22.01	14.08	7.77	10.22	15.10	13.95	3.30	0.96	6.35
South Down	72,072	1.84	3.22	19.32	9.93	14.17	8.17	14.07	15.60	4.84	1.39	7.46
Strangford	70,645	2.63	4.22	21.69	14.03	9.66	9.36	15.18	13.41	2.50	1.11	6.21
Upper Bann	72,091	2.13	2.87	18.38	10.50	7.94	10.37	17.76	18.28	3.78	1.38	6.63
West Tyrone	59,492	1.32	2.36	16.44	8.57	12.02	8.09	14.01	20.02	7.58	2.15	7.45
NUTS Level III												
Belfast	197,519	1.75	5.40	17.97	10.77	4.06	7.86	15.94	16.66	6.21	2.31	11.06
Outer Belfast	263,371	3.04	4.86	23.59	14.18	6.66	9.05	15.26	12.45	2.83	1.09	6.99
East of Northern Ireland	281,328	2.26	3.26	19.74	11.59	9.96	9.89	16.20	15.88	3.61	1.24	6.37
North of Northern Ireland	191,922	1.67	2.82	17.23	9.31	9.11	8.68	15.46	18.80	6.08	2.37	8.46
West and South of Northern Ireland	252,939	1.59	2.72	17.15	8.93	12.87	8.00	14.31	18.47	6.56	1.74	7.65

Notes:
1 For Long-term unemployed year last worked is 1999 or earlier.
2 In the NS–SeC classification, all full-time students are recorded in the 'full-time students' category regardless of whether they are economically active or not.

Table KS14b: National Statistics – Socio Economic Classification – Males

Area	All males aged 16-74	Percentage of males aged 16-74:										
		Large employers and higher managerial occupations	Higher professional occupations	Lower managerial and professional occupations	Intermediate occupations	Small employers and own account workers	Lower supervisory and technical occupations	Semi-routine occupations	Routine occupations	Never worked	Long-term unemployed[1]	Full-time students[2]
Northern Ireland	**581,232**	**3.17**	**5.34**	**17.69**	**6.51**	**14.11**	**12.40**	**10.34**	**17.58**	**3.29**	**2.36**	**7.21**
Local Government District												
Antrim	17,508	4.22	4.38	20.05	8.23	14.01	13.60	9.61	15.94	3.25	1.33	5.39
Ards	25,943	3.76	5.30	19.01	8.58	16.22	14.08	9.25	14.96	1.51	1.54	5.79
Armagh	18,914	2.47	4.06	16.03	5.53	19.17	11.33	8.41	20.01	3.83	2.36	6.82
Ballymena	20,581	3.66	4.32	17.26	5.43	16.16	14.39	12.39	17.79	1.69	1.40	5.52
Ballymoney	9,421	2.13	3.52	12.91	4.22	21.59	11.60	11.97	22.44	2.46	1.82	5.33
Banbridge	14,692	3.28	5.00	16.91	6.91	19.17	12.69	8.53	18.57	1.89	1.33	5.72
Belfast	92,638	2.56	7.59	16.86	6.43	6.62	11.57	12.47	17.19	4.73	3.58	10.39
Carrickfergus	13,133	3.45	5.77	20.73	9.35	8.62	16.23	10.85	15.36	1.53	1.80	6.30
Castlereagh	22,526	4.90	9.24	24.36	9.08	9.12	12.87	9.78	12.20	1.37	1.14	5.94
Coleraine	19,112	2.82	5.56	18.01	7.26	15.49	11.01	10.74	15.23	2.46	2.36	9.06
Cookstown	11,191	2.14	3.22	12.22	3.44	23.05	11.67	8.77	23.10	3.88	1.87	6.64
Craigavon	27,704	3.12	3.94	16.28	5.72	12.45	14.26	13.98	19.52	2.51	2.09	6.14
Derry	35,290	2.82	4.24	18.18	5.97	9.80	12.48	10.62	17.83	5.16	4.49	8.41
Down	22,149	3.10	4.90	18.77	6.36	20.01	11.45	7.56	16.53	2.75	1.63	6.95
Dungannon	16,396	2.62	3.68	12.81	3.90	20.88	10.76	9.95	22.84	4.01	1.86	6.68
Fermanagh	20,222	2.12	4.05	13.36	5.94	20.13	10.72	10.03	20.23	4.19	2.85	6.37
Larne	10,940	2.93	4.20	16.63	6.39	13.11	17.58	12.01	18.22	2.04	2.06	4.84
Limavady	11,690	2.63	2.76	15.20	7.78	16.07	12.87	9.89	19.59	4.45	3.02	5.74
Lisburn	37,191	4.60	6.39	21.81	7.63	11.95	12.04	9.89	14.84	2.38	1.61	6.87
Magherafelt	13,925	2.44	3.68	12.46	3.42	23.96	12.24	9.08	21.96	3.02	1.50	6.24
Moyle	5,508	1.78	3.81	13.74	4.03	23.98	10.80	9.89	19.15	3.70	2.87	6.23
Newry and Mourne	29,571	1.98	3.62	13.99	3.30	20.59	11.00	8.57	22.42	4.94	3.06	6.53
Newtownabbey	28,012	3.99	5.78	20.94	7.93	9.44	15.26	10.72	15.69	1.51	1.48	7.26
North Down	26,908	6.05	8.34	26.59	10.14	10.30	11.28	8.25	9.06	1.52	1.33	7.14
Omagh	16,768	2.29	3.88	15.90	6.02	20.74	10.30	8.26	18.18	5.03	2.53	6.86
Strabane	13,299	1.56	2.57	11.62	4.26	18.57	11.25	9.40	25.52	5.72	3.36	6.16
Health and Social Services Board												
Eastern	227,355	3.73	7.12	20.00	7.57	10.58	12.02	10.43	15.03	3.07	2.33	8.13
Northern	149,331	3.22	4.67	17.40	6.41	15.55	13.71	10.68	17.80	2.36	1.74	6.47
Southern	107,277	2.64	3.98	15.16	4.90	18.09	12.09	10.15	20.78	3.55	2.27	6.39
Western	97,269	2.39	3.74	15.53	5.96	15.79	11.62	9.84	19.65	4.93	3.48	7.09

© Crown copyright 2002

Area	All males aged 16-74	Percentage of males aged 16-74:										
		Large employers and higher managerial occupations	Higher professional occupations	Lower managerial and professional occupations	Intermediate occupations	Small employers and own account workers	Lower supervisory and technical occupations	Semi-routine occupations	Routine occupations	Never worked	Long-term unemployed[1]	Full-time students[2]
Education and Library Board												
Belfast	92,638	2.56	7.59	16.86	6.43	6.62	11.57	12.47	17.19	4.73	3.58	10.39
North Eastern	138,140	3.30	4.78	17.82	6.65	14.94	13.88	10.83	17.37	2.24	1.73	6.45
South Eastern	134,717	4.53	6.80	22.15	8.35	13.29	12.33	9.04	13.55	1.93	1.46	6.57
Southern	118,468	2.59	3.91	14.88	4.76	18.56	12.05	10.02	21.00	3.58	2.23	6.41
Western	97,269	2.39	3.74	15.53	5.96	15.79	11.62	9.84	19.65	4.93	3.48	7.09
Parliamentary Constituency												
Belfast East	26,549	3.97	8.05	21.85	8.31	7.21	13.36	11.84	15.27	2.41	1.99	5.74
Belfast North	27,751	1.84	4.13	14.24	5.87	7.05	13.70	14.90	22.27	5.17	4.18	6.63
Belfast South	33,831	3.83	14.03	21.08	6.96	6.38	8.53	8.58	10.16	2.41	1.83	16.20
Belfast West	27,302	1.28	2.34	11.95	5.72	6.78	12.78	15.04	21.71	7.97	5.82	8.60
East Antrim	29,530	3.55	5.85	19.44	7.84	10.13	16.09	11.08	15.91	1.62	1.76	6.74
East Londonderry	30,802	2.75	4.50	16.94	7.46	15.71	11.72	10.41	16.88	3.22	2.61	7.80
Fermanagh and South Tyrone	31,909	2.37	4.05	13.33	5.34	20.41	10.62	10.15	20.86	4.06	2.42	6.38
Foyle	35,290	2.82	4.24	18.18	5.97	9.80	12.48	10.62	17.83	5.16	4.49	8.41
Lagan Valley	35,869	4.97	6.89	22.90	7.89	13.34	12.13	9.09	14.25	1.55	0.98	6.01
Mid Ulster	29,825	2.29	3.36	12.23	3.35	23.13	11.92	8.94	22.87	3.56	1.77	6.58
Newry and Armagh	34,725	2.02	3.63	14.88	4.58	17.84	11.24	8.87	21.96	5.09	3.07	6.82
North Antrim	35,510	2.97	4.03	15.56	4.89	18.81	13.09	11.89	19.23	2.21	1.74	5.58
North Down	30,191	5.84	8.08	26.02	9.82	10.83	11.67	8.33	9.65	1.52	1.39	6.87
South Antrim	35,749	4.17	4.89	21.25	8.33	12.27	14.62	9.65	15.34	2.31	1.24	5.94
South Down	36,154	2.70	4.38	16.47	4.89	23.33	11.11	7.63	18.22	2.93	1.80	6.56
Strangford	34,647	4.01	5.99	19.93	8.70	15.12	13.74	9.22	14.30	1.43	1.42	6.14
Upper Bann	35,531	3.22	4.19	16.79	6.20	12.69	14.04	12.89	19.55	2.39	1.94	6.11
West Tyrone	30,067	1.97	3.30	14.01	5.24	19.78	10.72	8.76	21.43	5.34	2.90	6.55
NUTS Level III												
Belfast	92,638	2.56	7.59	16.86	6.43	6.62	11.57	12.47	17.19	4.73	3.58	10.39
Outer Belfast	127,770	4.70	7.10	22.96	8.66	10.21	13.17	9.80	13.40	1.74	1.46	6.79
East of Northern Ireland	139,517	3.46	4.59	17.89	6.80	15.85	13.81	10.57	17.29	2.23	1.63	5.87
North of Northern Ireland	94,320	2.49	3.99	16.07	5.93	14.97	11.87	10.47	19.14	4.25	3.35	7.46
West and South of Northern Ireland	126,987	2.26	3.77	13.97	4.51	20.95	11.08	8.99	21.21	4.24	2.42	6.59

Notes:
1 For Long-term unemployed year last worked is 1999 or earlier.
2 In the NS-SeC classification, all full-time students are recorded in the 'full-time students' category regardless of whether they are economically active or not.

KS14b

Table KS14c: National Statistics – Socio Economic Classification – Females

Area	All females aged 16-74	Large employers and higher managerial occupations	Higher professional occupations	Lower managerial and professional occupations	Intermediate occupations	Small employers and own account workers	Lower supervisory and technical occupations	Semi-routine occupations	Routine occupations	Never worked	Long-term unemployed[1]	Full-time students[2]
					Percentage of females aged 16-74:							
Northern Ireland	**605,847**	**1.09**	**2.29**	**20.93**	**15.49**	**3.57**	**5.28**	**20.30**	**15.02**	**6.44**	**1.01**	**8.57**
Local Government District												
Antrim	17,071	1.27	2.16	22.41	17.60	3.59	6.29	19.84	14.23	5.16	0.73	6.72
Ards	26,935	1.16	2.30	21.85	18.49	4.73	5.40	22.02	13.08	3.88	0.90	6.19
Armagh	18,838	1.43	1.53	21.34	15.77	4.71	4.81	18.19	15.65	6.95	0.94	8.67
Ballymena	21,367	0.88	1.80	21.21	15.55	3.97	5.77	23.90	14.63	4.92	0.84	6.52
Ballymoney	9,466	0.71	1.50	18.35	13.52	4.62	5.95	22.87	17.63	6.68	0.91	7.27
Banbridge	14,591	1.07	2.11	22.40	15.37	4.78	5.52	20.68	15.35	4.72	0.82	7.20
Belfast	104,881	1.04	3.46	18.94	14.59	1.80	4.59	19.01	16.20	7.52	1.18	11.66
Carrickfergus	13,818	1.15	1.96	22.07	19.54	3.01	6.20	21.64	13.73	3.63	0.64	6.43
Castlereagh	24,629	1.71	3.78	27.37	20.68	3.01	4.22	19.47	10.30	2.91	0.59	5.94
Coleraine	20,977	0.87	2.39	20.53	13.94	4.61	5.38	20.61	12.36	5.94	1.13	12.24
Cookstown	11,226	0.85	1.39	18.70	12.28	4.64	4.93	20.63	17.23	9.38	0.84	9.14
Craigavon	28,601	1.06	1.50	19.41	14.70	3.10	7.05	22.89	17.10	5.42	0.81	6.97
Derry	37,375	0.99	1.76	18.19	12.08	2.27	5.52	19.59	20.13	8.00	1.76	9.73
Down	22,100	1.11	2.11	23.31	16.23	4.95	5.52	19.68	12.32	5.78	0.96	8.03
Dungannon	16,439	0.87	1.78	20.43	13.62	4.88	5.03	19.61	15.46	8.92	0.87	8.53
Fermanagh	19,676	0.87	1.65	19.25	12.76	5.64	5.08	20.66	15.08	9.09	1.17	8.75
Larne	11,146	0.89	1.74	21.16	15.95	4.45	6.80	22.39	14.48	4.93	0.82	6.39
Limavady	11,071	0.87	1.22	17.50	12.78	3.55	5.20	20.67	20.53	8.76	1.07	7.85
Lisburn	39,285	1.47	2.49	23.18	17.97	3.46	5.05	20.51	12.41	5.07	0.86	7.53
Magherafelt	13,499	0.72	1.60	21.35	13.53	4.36	4.69	19.11	17.49	7.52	1.01	8.62
Moyle	5,565	0.84	1.71	21.51	12.31	5.25	5.39	20.09	14.39	9.09	1.40	8.01
Newry and Mourne	29,997	0.90	1.71	19.56	12.92	4.24	4.97	20.20	15.77	9.98	1.12	8.63
Newtownabbey	29,895	1.25	2.43	21.57	20.02	2.69	5.56	21.21	12.85	3.77	0.71	7.94
North Down	27,974	1.70	2.93	26.63	19.45	4.19	5.25	19.55	9.04	3.14	0.79	7.33
Omagh	16,277	0.59	1.82	22.32	12.63	4.76	4.63	19.17	14.09	9.77	1.27	8.96
Strabane	13,148	0.75	0.87	14.71	11.14	3.27	6.37	19.60	24.13	9.99	1.54	7.63
Health and Social Services Board												
Eastern	245,804	1.27	3.03	22.05	16.87	3.07	4.87	19.75	13.50	5.61	0.97	9.01
Northern	154,030	0.99	1.98	21.06	16.16	3.88	5.69	21.31	14.45	5.56	0.86	8.05
Southern	108,466	1.05	1.69	20.34	14.32	4.19	5.57	20.53	16.00	7.38	0.93	7.99
Western	97,547	0.85	1.57	18.55	12.26	3.64	5.36	19.86	18.69	8.87	1.45	8.91

Table KS14c: National Statistics – Socio Economic Classification – Females (continued)

KS14c

Area	All females aged 16-74	Percentage of females aged 16-74:										
		Large employers and higher managerial occupations	Higher professional occupations	Lower managerial and professional occupations	Intermediate occupations	Small employers and own account workers	Lower supervisory and technical occupations	Semi-routine occupations	Routine occupations	Never worked	Long-term unemployed[1]	Full-time students[2]
Education and Library Board												
Belfast	104,881	1.04	3.46	18.94	14.59	1.80	4.59	19.01	16.20	7.52	1.18	11.66
North Eastern	142,804	1.00	2.03	21.24	16.46	3.83	5.75	21.36	14.24	5.26	0.86	7.97
South Eastern	140,923	1.44	2.71	24.36	18.56	4.00	5.09	20.30	11.49	4.19	0.82	7.03
Southern	119,692	1.03	1.66	20.19	14.13	4.23	5.51	20.54	16.11	7.57	0.92	8.10
Western	97,547	0.85	1.57	18.55	12.26	3.64	5.36	19.86	18.69	8.87	1.45	8.91
Parliamentary Constituency												
Belfast East	29,420	1.31	3.33	23.60	18.95	2.51	4.81	20.97	13.19	4.69	0.88	5.76
Belfast North	31,752	0.72	1.66	15.34	14.36	1.54	5.65	23.19	20.52	8.72	1.43	6.88
Belfast South	38,073	1.63	6.70	25.40	14.11	2.27	3.45	13.18	9.22	4.20	0.65	19.20
Belfast West	31,516	0.53	0.99	12.57	14.30	1.18	4.74	21.88	21.32	11.60	1.76	9.12
East Antrim	30,870	1.20	2.23	21.97	17.92	3.41	6.18	21.21	13.52	3.97	0.69	7.70
East Londonderry	32,048	0.87	1.98	19.48	13.54	4.25	5.32	20.63	15.18	6.92	1.11	10.72
Fermanagh and South Tyrone	31,325	0.87	1.74	19.71	13.04	5.59	5.06	20.41	15.18	8.86	1.04	8.50
Foyle	37,375	0.99	1.76	18.19	12.08	2.27	5.52	19.59	20.13	8.00	1.76	9.73
Lagan Valley	36,909	1.63	2.75	25.18	18.61	3.98	5.17	19.98	11.76	3.67	0.58	6.70
Mid Ulster	29,515	0.79	1.51	20.17	13.11	4.30	4.84	19.63	17.11	8.63	0.94	8.98
Newry and Armagh	35,107	1.20	1.52	19.92	14.09	4.22	4.91	18.77	16.30	9.35	1.09	8.64
North Antrim	36,398	0.83	1.71	20.51	14.53	4.34	5.76	23.05	15.37	6.01	0.95	6.95
North Down	31,489	1.65	2.84	25.93	19.26	4.35	5.29	20.05	9.40	3.21	0.79	7.21
South Antrim	36,149	1.26	2.25	22.76	19.77	3.32	5.86	20.49	12.57	4.27	0.69	6.76
South Down	35,918	0.98	2.05	22.20	15.00	4.94	5.20	20.56	12.96	6.77	0.98	8.36
Strangford	35,998	1.31	2.53	23.38	19.17	4.40	5.13	20.91	12.55	3.53	0.81	6.27
Upper Bann	36,560	1.06	1.58	19.92	14.69	3.32	6.79	22.49	17.04	5.14	0.83	7.13
West Tyrone	29,425	0.66	1.39	18.92	11.96	4.09	5.41	19.36	18.58	9.87	1.39	8.36
NUTS Level III												
Belfast	104,881	1.04	3.46	18.94	14.59	1.80	4.59	19.01	16.20	7.52	1.18	11.66
Outer Belfast	135,601	1.48	2.75	24.18	19.38	3.31	5.17	20.39	11.56	3.85	0.74	7.18
East of Northern Ireland	141,811	1.07	1.95	21.56	16.30	4.17	6.04	21.74	14.49	4.97	0.85	6.87
North of Northern Ireland	97,602	0.88	1.68	18.35	12.58	3.45	5.60	20.28	18.48	7.85	1.41	9.44
West and South of Northern Ireland	125,952	0.91	1.66	20.36	13.38	4.73	4.89	19.68	15.70	8.91	1.05	8.73

Notes:
1 For Long-term unemployed year last worked is 1999 or earlier.
2 In the NS-SeC classification, all full-time students are recorded in the 'full-time students' category regardless of whether they are economically active or not.

Table KS15: Travel to Work

Area	All persons aged 16-74 in employment	Percentage of persons aged 16-74 in employment who work mainly at or from home	Percentage of persons aged 16-74 in employment who usually travel to work by:										Percentage of public transport[2] users in households:	
			Train	Bus, minibus or coach	Motorcycle, scooter or moped	Driving a car or van	Passenger in a car or van	Car or van pool	Taxi	Bicycle	On foot	Other method[1]	With a car or van[3]	Without a car or van[3]
Northern Ireland	**686,644**	**8.80**	**0.86**	**6.01**	**0.80**	**55.88**	**8.98**	**5.73**	**1.58**	**0.87**	**9.73**	**0.75**	**69.92**	**29.60**
Local Government District														
Antrim	22,438	9.05	0.47	4.63	0.76	54.23	9.60	6.23	1.53	1.93	10.72	0.84	66.20	25.68
Ards	33,268	9.08	0.20	5.32	1.22	61.32	8.14	5.84	0.37	0.57	7.33	0.60	75.52	24.43
Armagh	22,302	13.14	0.48	2.17	0.58	59.87	8.47	6.03	0.49	0.34	7.36	1.09	84.89	15.11
Ballymena	26,499	9.64	0.28	2.30	0.77	59.84	10.43	5.82	0.74	0.87	8.54	0.76	75.00	24.85
Ballymoney	11,275	12.83	0.45	2.29	0.45	58.41	10.82	6.12	0.20	0.47	6.87	1.08	83.50	16.50
Banbridge	18,758	11.75	0.28	3.72	0.62	60.28	9.04	5.90	0.70	0.30	6.51	0.88	78.96	21.04
Belfast	100,826	4.49	0.61	15.31	0.91	44.58	7.81	4.64	3.99	1.42	15.86	0.37	59.33	40.31
Carrickfergus	17,176	5.16	5.53	3.91	1.42	58.81	9.22	6.38	2.09	0.67	6.26	0.56	76.33	23.67
Castlereagh	30,244	5.84	0.23	9.88	1.22	62.13	6.85	5.49	0.77	0.96	6.30	0.33	78.74	21.06
Coleraine	23,156	10.32	0.63	2.79	0.92	55.83	8.96	6.22	1.24	1.14	11.26	0.68	63.10	35.89
Cookstown	12,382	14.71	0.12	1.80	0.52	57.16	9.95	6.35	0.31	0.47	7.53	1.08	84.87	14.71
Craigavon	32,993	7.40	1.69	3.99	1.29	55.62	10.98	5.69	1.98	1.44	9.34	0.57	70.24	29.76
Derry	36,225	6.03	0.20	6.67	0.51	52.26	10.71	6.56	3.43	0.55	12.45	0.63	64.48	35.07
Down	26,881	10.35	0.12	4.04	0.49	58.16	9.45	5.90	0.42	0.71	9.40	0.96	82.63	17.37
Dungannon	18,461	14.00	0.16	2.09	0.35	59.31	9.46	5.62	0.73	0.36	6.51	1.40	84.82	14.94
Fermanagh	22,782	15.32	0.11	2.05	0.43	59.71	8.16	5.05	0.94	0.42	6.90	0.90	81.67	18.13
Larne	13,467	8.90	1.57	3.19	0.82	56.36	9.33	6.49	0.55	0.57	11.17	1.06	72.97	26.56
Limavady	12,945	9.45	0.17	3.75	0.50	54.04	11.66	7.71	0.92	1.03	9.52	1.26	82.05	17.36
Lisburn	47,400	7.47	2.07	5.90	0.99	57.86	7.61	5.21	2.02	1.11	9.13	0.64	74.62	25.30
Magherafelt	16,477	12.72	0.14	2.74	0.29	58.15	10.26	6.28	0.33	0.34	7.68	1.07	83.54	16.46
Moyle	5,949	15.60	0.17	2.42	0.54	54.08	9.43	6.52	0.45	0.42	9.46	0.91	75.32	24.68
Newry and Mourne	31,873	10.98	0.58	2.97	0.38	56.73	10.44	6.36	0.99	0.46	8.88	1.22	83.77	16.05
Newtownabbey	36,291	5.50	0.80	9.75	1.04	59.09	9.24	5.55	1.27	0.63	6.65	0.48	75.60	24.06
North Down	34,629	7.31	3.38	3.21	1.11	60.08	7.41	5.71	1.04	1.00	9.24	0.50	76.02	23.37
Omagh	18,606	13.80	0.16	2.34	0.32	57.10	8.24	5.32	0.51	0.61	10.08	1.52	83.05	15.67
Strabane	13,341	13.15	0.12	3.25	0.46	52.26	10.10	6.36	1.44	0.64	11.03	1.18	72.83	27.17
Health and Social Services Board														
Eastern	273,248	6.65	1.08	9.22	0.98	54.17	7.82	5.24	2.12	1.09	11.12	0.52	66.83	32.88
Northern	185,110	9.37	1.01	4.33	0.82	57.56	9.66	6.08	1.01	0.83	8.54	0.78	74.26	24.53
Southern	124,387	10.98	0.75	3.08	0.69	57.92	9.87	5.94	1.08	0.66	8.02	1.00	77.92	22.02
Western	103,899	10.80	0.16	4.08	0.45	54.98	9.75	6.12	1.79	0.60	10.26	1.00	71.24	28.28

© Crown copyright 2002

Area	All persons aged 16-74 in employment	Percentage of persons aged 16-74 in employment who work mainly at or from home	Percentage of persons aged 16-74 in employment who usually travel to work by:										Percentage of public transport[2] users in households:	
			Train	Bus, minibus or coach	Motorcycle, scooter or moped	Driving a car or van	Passenger in a car or van	Car or van pool	Taxi	Bicycle	On foot	Other method[1]	With a car or van[3]	Without a car or van[3]
Education and Library Board														
Belfast	100,826	4.49	0.61	15.31	0.91	44.58	7.81	4.64	3.99	1.42	15.86	0.37	59.33	40.31
North Eastern	172,728	8.99	1.08	4.51	0.84	57.59	9.64	6.07	1.06	0.86	8.61	0.76	74.00	24.78
South Eastern	172,422	7.91	1.35	5.65	1.02	59.77	7.83	5.59	1.04	0.89	8.35	0.60	76.81	22.99
Southern	136,769	11.32	0.69	2.96	0.67	57.85	9.88	5.98	1.01	0.64	7.98	1.01	78.25	21.67
Western	103,899	10.80	0.16	4.08	0.45	54.98	9.75	6.12	1.79	0.60	10.26	1.00	71.24	28.28
Parliamentary Constituency														
Belfast East	32,555	5.13	0.44	12.36	1.23	54.49	7.74	4.96	1.27	1.58	10.46	0.33	67.78	32.17
Belfast North	27,898	4.20	0.54	18.94	1.12	42.66	9.69	4.85	3.83	0.94	12.79	0.45	56.06	43.88
Belfast South	42,633	4.90	0.84	11.07	0.76	50.52	6.58	4.66	1.79	1.75	16.86	0.26	63.12	35.86
Belfast West	24,946	3.30	0.44	19.43	0.69	35.48	8.68	4.69	10.52	0.72	15.55	0.48	59.65	40.29
East Antrim	37,785	6.46	3.45	4.26	1.17	58.31	9.25	6.26	1.39	0.65	8.07	0.73	74.96	24.49
East Londonderry	36,101	10.01	0.47	3.14	0.77	55.19	9.92	6.76	1.12	1.10	10.64	0.89	70.48	28.67
Fermanagh and South Tyrone	36,315	15.08	0.12	2.01	0.41	59.55	8.35	5.20	0.88	0.40	6.89	1.12	83.07	16.67
Foyle	36,225	6.03	0.20	6.67	0.51	52.26	10.71	6.56	3.43	0.55	12.45	0.63	64.48	35.07
Lagan Valley	47,659	8.33	2.03	4.31	1.02	60.33	7.33	5.22	0.91	1.09	8.75	0.67	79.05	20.85
Mid Ulster	33,787	13.37	0.15	2.35	0.38	57.98	10.36	6.27	0.36	0.38	7.31	1.10	83.89	16.00
Newry and Armagh	38,146	11.61	0.62	2.47	0.49	58.02	9.37	6.14	0.88	0.40	8.90	1.10	82.53	17.30
North Antrim	43,723	11.27	0.31	2.31	0.66	58.69	10.39	5.99	0.56	0.70	8.24	0.86	77.33	22.58
North Down	38,677	7.53	3.08	3.38	1.12	60.17	7.53	5.70	0.97	0.96	9.05	0.50	75.58	23.82
South Antrim	47,022	7.43	0.40	7.21	0.87	57.92	9.19	5.92	1.19	1.18	8.01	0.66	76.77	20.63
South Down	43,035	12.03	0.22	3.55	0.42	57.60	9.78	6.08	0.47	0.59	8.11	1.16	84.21	15.79
Strangford	45,358	8.64	0.19	6.32	1.18	61.68	7.56	5.75	0.41	0.58	7.09	0.59	77.80	22.09
Upper Bann	42,832	7.61	1.36	4.03	1.14	56.45	10.79	5.87	1.79	1.20	9.18	0.58	70.94	29.06
West Tyrone	31,947	13.53	0.14	2.72	0.38	55.08	9.02	5.75	0.90	0.63	10.47	1.38	78.03	21.31
NUTS Level III														
Belfast	100,826	4.49	0.61	15.31	0.91	44.58	7.81	4.64	3.99	1.42	15.86	0.37	59.33	40.31
Outer Belfast	165,740	6.47	2.09	6.70	1.11	59.47	7.95	5.56	1.43	0.91	7.79	0.51	76.15	23.60
East of Northern Ireland	174,304	9.31	0.63	3.98	0.90	58.12	9.60	5.93	0.94	0.95	8.86	0.77	74.02	24.76
North of Northern Ireland	102,891	9.65	0.31	4.26	0.59	54.07	10.29	6.55	1.83	0.74	10.85	0.86	68.55	30.99
West and South of Northern Ireland	142,883	13.29	0.29	2.37	0.41	58.28	9.29	5.86	0.67	0.43	7.92	1.18	83.74	15.97

KS15

55

Notes:
1 'Other method' includes no fixed place of work, working at offshore installation, working outside the UK.
2 For purposes of this table, public transport is defined as: train, bus, minibus or coach.
3 The last two columns show the number of persons who travel to work by public transport who live in a household with/without a car or van expressed as a percentage of the number of persons who travel to work by public transport. Note that these columns may not sum up to 100% as residents of communal establishments who travel to work by public transport appear in neither column.

Table KS16: Dwellings, Household Spaces and Accommodation Type

Area	All dwellings			All household spaces		With no residents		Percentage of all household spaces which are of accommodation type:						
	All dwellings	Unshared Dwelling	Shared dwelling	All household spaces	With residents	Vacant	Second residence/ holiday accommodation	Detached house or bungalow	Semi-detached house or bungalow	Terraced (including end-terraced) house or bungalow	Purpose built block of flats or tenement	Part of a converted or shared house (includes bed-sits)	In commercial building[1]	Caravan or other mobile or temporary structure
Northern Ireland	**658,351**	**658,317**	**34**	**658,426**	**626,718**	**26,716**	**4,992**	**36.47**	**27.32**	**27.39**	**7.17**	**1.02**	**0.34**	**0.28**
Local Government District														
Antrim	17,652	17,652	–	17,652	17,178	455	19	40.41	22.78	29.84	6.07	0.36	0.22	0.32
Ards	30,068	30,068	–	30,068	28,689	978	401	39.13	27.93	26.07	6.00	0.45	0.25	0.17
Armagh	19,558	19,558	–	19,560	18,471	1,057	32	52.21	23.19	19.45	3.13	0.54	0.48	1.01
Ballymena	23,034	23,031	3	23,033	22,059	930	44	45.63	23.96	23.46	5.92	0.61	0.20	0.23
Ballymoney	9,914	9,914	–	9,914	9,635	259	20	52.05	32.34	12.03	2.57	0.36	0.21	0.43
Banbridge	15,891	15,891	–	15,891	15,188	658	45	50.43	21.89	21.93	4.43	0.38	0.40	0.53
Belfast	119,553	119,537	16	119,584	113,934	5,314	336	11.13	28.67	46.07	11.15	2.62	0.32	0.04
Carrickfergus	15,560	15,560	–	15,560	14,785	725	50	35.38	26.69	27.46	9.61	0.49	0.24	0.12
Castlereagh	27,518	27,518	–	27,518	26,887	602	29	26.75	41.39	20.21	11.24	0.25	0.11	0.05
Coleraine	24,306	24,301	5	24,317	21,583	1,192	1,542	43.97	24.48	21.41	7.80	1.63	0.59	0.12
Cookstown	11,396	11,396	–	11,396	10,883	481	32	56.66	21.47	17.93	2.69	0.33	0.24	0.68
Craigavon	31,717	31,717	–	31,717	30,182	1,505	30	32.51	25.47	34.54	6.28	0.67	0.18	0.35
Derry	37,326	37,323	3	37,332	35,947	1,317	68	26.07	29.94	34.32	8.07	1.17	0.33	0.09
Down	23,710	23,707	3	23,709	22,329	930	450	51.54	21.32	21.22	4.27	0.57	0.68	0.41
Dungannon	17,195	17,195	–	17,195	16,259	907	29	51.43	26.96	17.27	2.71	0.34	0.62	0.68
Fermanagh	22,201	22,201	–	22,201	20,454	1,273	474	60.69	19.35	14.30	3.33	0.80	0.76	0.78
Larne	13,254	13,254	–	13,254	12,250	831	173	36.33	22.22	31.94	8.20	0.79	0.35	0.17
Limavady	11,132	11,132	–	11,132	10,697	398	37	47.92	27.86	19.26	3.41	0.68	0.49	0.38
Lisburn	41,140	41,140	–	41,140	39,862	1,240	38	36.66	28.80	25.72	7.97	0.44	0.17	0.25
Magherafelt	13,553	13,553	–	13,553	12,957	582	14	55.75	23.27	17.19	2.39	0.29	0.48	0.63
Moyle	6,884	6,884	–	6,884	5,888	418	578	54.13	27.00	14.09	3.14	0.51	0.97	0.16
Newry and Mourne	31,004	31,004	–	31,004	29,314	1,424	266	45.53	30.20	18.75	3.80	0.79	0.27	0.66
Newtownabbey	32,137	32,137	–	32,137	31,302	788	47	31.89	31.43	25.19	11.02	0.28	0.13	0.06
North Down	32,208	32,205	3	32,219	30,888	1,178	153	37.38	32.35	18.51	9.85	1.48	0.33	0.11
Omagh	17,086	17,082	4	17,097	16,123	928	46	57.10	20.05	17.45	3.57	0.82	0.63	0.38
Strabane	13,357	13,357	–	13,359	12,974	346	39	50.53	22.92	23.12	2.01	0.51	0.28	0.63
Health and Social Services Board														
Eastern	274,194	274,175	19	274,238	262,589	10,242	1,407	26.18	29.68	32.84	9.37	1.50	0.30	0.13
Northern	167,688	167,682	6	167,700	158,520	6,661	2,519	42.82	25.85	23.27	6.89	0.61	0.32	0.25
Southern	115,365	115,365	–	115,367	109,414	5,551	402	44.64	26.08	23.43	4.29	0.59	0.35	0.62
Western	101,103	101,095	8	101,121	96,195	4,262	664	44.55	24.79	23.93	4.95	0.89	0.49	0.39

Table KS16: Dwellings, Household Spaces and Accommodation Type (continued)

Area	All dwellings			All household spaces		With no residents		Percentage of all household spaces which are of accommodation type:						
	All dwellings	Unshared Dwelling	Shared dwelling	All household spaces	With residents	Vacant	Second residence/ holiday accommodation	Detached house or bungalow	Semi-detached house or bungalow	Terraced (including end-terraced) house or bungalow	Purpose built block of flats or tenement	Part of a converted or shared house (includes bed-sits)	In commercial building[1]	Caravan or other mobile or temporary structure
Education and Library Board														
Belfast	119,553	119,537	16	119,584	113,934	5,314	336	11.13	28.67	46.07	11.15	2.62	0.32	0.04
North Eastern	156,292	156,286	6	156,304	147,637	6,180	2,487	41.81	26.17	23.65	7.20	0.63	0.32	0.22
South Eastern	154,641	154,638	3	154,654	148,655	4,928	1,071	37.81	30.46	22.62	7.99	0.64	0.29	0.19
Southern	126,764	126,761	3	126,763	120,297	6,032	434	45.72	25.67	22.93	4.15	0.57	0.34	0.62
Western	101,103	101,095	8	101,121	96,195	4,262	664	44.55	24.79	23.93	4.95	0.89	0.49	0.39
Parliamentary Constituency														
Belfast East	36,244	36,241	3	36,245	34,824	1,384	37	15.16	35.22	36.26	11.99	1.13	0.22	0.02
Belfast North	38,073	38,073	-	38,075	36,383	1,646	46	10.36	28.67	45.12	13.90	1.63	0.31	0.01
Belfast South	42,355	42,341	14	42,382	39,715	2,404	263	15.01	26.40	40.43	12.95	4.79	0.41	-
Belfast West	31,535	31,535	-	31,535	30,992	527	16	7.66	31.77	50.47	9.27	0.55	0.16	0.13
East Antrim	34,782	34,782	-	34,782	32,789	1,747	246	36.63	23.99	29.55	8.86	0.58	0.28	0.12
East Londonderry	35,438	35,433	5	35,449	32,280	1,590	1,579	45.21	25.54	20.74	6.42	1.33	0.56	0.20
Fermanagh and South Tyrone	34,690	34,690	-	34,690	32,203	1,989	498	57.21	21.82	15.62	3.25	0.66	0.76	0.67
Foyle	37,326	37,323	3	37,332	35,947	1,317	68	26.07	29.94	34.32	8.07	1.17	0.33	0.09
Lagan Valley	39,829	39,829	-	39,829	38,405	1,378	46	41.81	27.50	22.77	6.99	0.40	0.22	0.32
Mid Ulster	29,655	29,655	-	29,655	28,350	1,254	51	55.58	23.47	17.19	2.38	0.28	0.34	0.75
Newry and Armagh	36,382	36,379	3	36,381	34,473	1,827	81	45.29	27.41	21.89	3.66	0.61	0.35	0.78
North Antrim	39,829	39,829	-	39,831	37,582	1,607	642	48.70	26.57	19.00	4.61	0.53	0.33	0.27
North Down	36,488	36,485	3	36,499	34,931	1,327	241	37.25	31.28	19.85	9.76	1.36	0.38	0.12
South Antrim	37,640	37,640	-	37,640	36,725	879	36	38.61	30.75	24.30	5.74	0.26	0.15	0.20
South Down	37,870	37,870	-	37,872	35,605	1,590	677	54.14	23.26	16.93	3.78	0.69	0.56	0.65
Strangford	39,400	39,400	-	39,400	37,898	1,166	336	39.59	29.85	23.68	6.17	0.39	0.16	0.15
Upper Bann	40,373	40,373	-	40,373	38,519	1,810	44	34.24	25.62	32.66	6.30	0.64	0.21	0.32
West Tyrone	30,444	30,439	5	30,456	29,097	1,274	85	54.22	21.31	19.94	2.88	0.69	0.48	0.49
NUTS Level III														
Belfast	119,553	119,537	16	119,584	113,934	5,314	336	11.13	28.67	46.07	11.15	2.62	0.32	0.04
Outer Belfast	148,563	148,560	3	148,574	143,724	4,533	317	33.81	32.25	23.20	9.81	0.60	0.19	0.13
East of Northern Ireland	155,320	155,320	-	155,324	147,875	6,287	1,162	41.70	24.14	27.18	5.82	0.55	0.31	0.31
North of Northern Ireland	102,920	102,911	9	102,938	96,724	3,930	2,284	40.21	27.55	24.69	5.85	1.02	0.44	0.24
West and South of Northern Ireland	131,994	131,989	5	132,006	124,461	6,652	893	53.35	24.13	17.51	3.21	0.61	0.49	0.70

Note:
1 'In commercial building' includes in an office building, or hotel, or over a shop.

Table KS17: Cars or Vans[1]

Area	All households	Percentage of households with:					All cars or vans in the area[2]
		No cars or vans	One car or van	Two cars or vans	Three cars or vans	Four or more cars or vans	
Northern Ireland	**626,718**	**26.32**	**44.45**	**23.60**	**4.28**	**1.36**	**691,662**
Local Government District							
Antrim	17,178	21.16	45.01	26.88	4.95	2.00	21,012
Ards	28,689	20.46	42.82	29.15	5.73	1.84	36,231
Armagh	18,471	18.02	44.58	28.68	6.41	2.31	24,226
Ballymena	22,059	21.23	44.05	27.19	5.54	1.98	27,291
Ballymoney	9,635	18.73	47.70	26.52	5.46	1.59	1,956
Banbridge	15,188	17.66	43.54	30.81	5.97	2.03	20,007
Belfast	113,934	43.78	40.79	13.08	1.92	0.43	84,978
Carrickfergus	14,785	23.06	46.25	26.17	3.81	0.72	6,713
Castlereagh	26,887	20.19	47.42	27.81	3.62	0.97	31,752
Coleraine	21,583	24.85	46.44	23.73	3.79	1.20	23,866
Cookstown	10,883	19.02	44.61	27.80	6.17	2.40	4,061
Craigavon	30,182	27.38	45.91	21.59	3.94	1.18	32,012
Derry	35,947	32.51	46.20	17.61	2.86	0.81	33,615
Down	22,329	19.13	44.58	28.64	5.65	1.99	28,454
Dungannon	16,259	19.26	45.54	27.08	5.94	2.18	20,674
Fermanagh	20,454	20.39	44.12	28.25	5.41	1.83	25,537
Larne	12,250	26.42	44.22	23.98	4.07	1.31	3,471
Limavady	10,697	21.99	47.79	24.18	4.49	1.56	2,456
Lisburn	39,862	22.06	44.55	27.24	4.71	1.46	47,593
Magherafelt	12,957	17.77	44.76	28.29	6.16	3.02	7,247
Moyle	5,888	23.37	47.71	23.37	4.26	1.29	6,644
Newry and Mourne	29,314	22.82	46.04	24.60	4.85	1.69	34,361
Newtownabbey	31,302	23.90	45.57	25.40	4.09	1.04	35,390
North Down	30,888	20.71	44.36	28.87	4.92	1.14	37,599
Omagh	16,123	20.60	45.05	26.29	5.91	2.14	20,095
Strabane	12,974	25.63	46.18	21.67	4.94	1.58	4,421
Health and Social Services Board							
Eastern	262,589	30.71	43.00	21.67	3.60	1.01	266,607
Northern	158,520	22.31	45.45	25.94	4.72	1.58	187,651
Southern	109,414	22.02	45.34	25.69	5.18	1.77	131,280
Western	96,195	25.84	45.74	22.61	4.38	1.44	106,124

Table KS17: Cars or Vans[1] (continued)

Area	All households	Percentage of households with:					All cars or vans in the area[2]
		No cars or vans	One car or van	Two cars or vans	Three cars or vans	Four or more cars or vans	
Education and Library Board							
Belfast	**113,934**	43.78	40.79	13.08	1.92	0.43	84,978
North Eastern	**147,637**	22.55	45.52	25.80	4.61	1.52	173,590
South Eastern	**148,655**	20.69	44.70	28.26	4.89	1.46	181,629
Southern	**120,297**	21.75	45.27	25.88	5.27	1.83	145,341
Western	**96,195**	25.84	45.74	22.61	4.38	1.44	106,124
Parliamentary Constituency							
Belfast East	**34,824**	32.79	45.53	18.64	2.62	0.42	32,189
Belfast North	**36,383**	49.17	39.56	9.66	1.35	0.26	23,298
Belfast South	**39,715**	34.11	42.43	19.74	2.90	0.83	37,428
Belfast West	**30,992**	50.94	39.53	8.26	1.05	0.23	18,647
East Antrim	**32,789**	23.98	44.97	26.16	3.95	0.95	37,105
East Londonderry	**32,280**	23.90	46.89	23.88	4.02	1.32	36,322
Fermanagh and South Tyrone	**32,203**	20.00	44.39	27.96	5.70	1.95	40,547
Foyle	**35,947**	32.51	46.20	17.61	2.86	0.81	33,615
Lagan Valley	**38,405**	18.02	44.82	30.14	5.34	1.69	49,312
Mid Ulster	**28,350**	18.46	45.10	27.76	6.02	2.66	36,972
Newry and Armagh	**34,473**	22.33	45.49	24.90	5.38	1.90	41,266
North Antrim	**37,582**	20.93	45.56	26.42	5.32	1.77	45,891
North Down	**34,931**	21.07	44.25	28.60	4.92	1.16	42,316
South Antrim	**36,725**	19.51	45.95	27.96	4.94	1.64	45,463
South Down	**35,605**	18.20	45.09	28.80	5.81	2.10	46,007
Strangford	**37,898**	19.10	43.25	30.26	5.56	1.83	48,664
Upper Bann	**38,519**	25.97	45.69	23.03	4.08	1.23	42,104
West Tyrone	**29,097**	22.84	45.56	24.23	5.48	1.89	34,516
NUTS Level III							
Belfast	**113,934**	43.78	40.79	13.08	1.92	0.43	84,978
Outer Belfast	**143,724**	21.92	45.44	27.19	4.32	1.13	169,047
East of Northern Ireland	**147,875**	22.07	44.35	26.72	5.12	1.74	178,478
North of Northern Ireland	**96,724**	26.78	46.67	21.49	3.87	1.19	102,958
West and South of Northern Ireland	**124,461**	20.10	45.06	27.01	5.71	2.13	156,201

KS17

Notes:
1 Includes any company car or van when available for private use.
2 'All cars or vans in area' includes only those cars and vans owned by, or available for use by, households. This count is not exact as households with more than 10 cars or vans are counted as having 10 cars or vans.

Table KS18: Tenure

Area	All households	Owner occupied		Shared ownership[1]	Rented from[2]:			Other[3]
		Owns outright	Owns with a mortgage or loan		Northern Ireland Housing Executive	Housing Association, Housing Co-operative or Charitable Trust	Private landlord or letting agency	
Northern Ireland	**626,718**	**29.37**	**39.44**	**0.79**	**18.59**	**2.63**	**6.65**	**2.54**
Local Government District								
Antrim	17,178	26.68	43.53	0.84	17.79	1.25	4.15	5.76
Ards	28,689	29.02	44.16	0.84	17.33	2.27	4.35	2.03
Armagh	18,471	36.86	39.57	0.43	12.94	1.30	6.22	2.66
Ballymena	22,059	33.79	39.84	0.55	16.36	1.72	5.05	2.69
Ballymoney	9,635	35.09	36.51	1.03	19.00	1.01	4.76	2.59
Banbridge	15,188	31.33	44.03	0.52	14.99	1.64	4.77	2.73
Belfast	113,934	24.05	31.02	1.01	26.35	4.74	11.04	1.78
Carrickfergus	14,785	23.50	50.61	1.10	16.62	2.54	4.06	1.56
Castlereagh	26,887	29.48	47.71	0.60	16.64	1.86	2.31	1.39
Coleraine	21,583	30.86	37.06	1.26	17.19	1.65	9.07	2.91
Cookstown	10,883	38.93	35.99	0.86	12.83	1.15	6.94	3.30
Craigavon	30,182	25.42	42.41	0.84	17.76	4.52	6.82	2.24
Derry	35,947	20.90	39.82	0.62	26.17	4.04	6.61	1.84
Down	22,329	32.71	40.22	0.70	14.55	1.78	6.61	3.43
Dungannon	16,259	37.23	35.94	0.33	14.12	1.49	7.46	3.42
Fermanagh	20,454	40.57	33.41	0.46	13.62	1.51	7.35	3.09
Larne	12,250	32.34	40.62	0.70	15.28	3.18	5.38	2.49
Limavady	10,697	30.58	39.13	0.66	17.66	1.72	5.54	4.70
Lisburn	39,862	25.79	44.38	0.81	20.38	2.77	2.91	2.96
Magherafelt	12,957	37.96	36.91	0.63	14.09	0.82	6.35	3.25
Moyle	5,888	37.04	30.35	0.51	18.67	1.89	8.24	3.31
Newry and Mourne	29,314	31.98	41.32	0.57	14.71	1.23	7.70	2.50
Newtownabbey	31,302	26.10	47.87	0.78	17.51	2.15	4.00	1.58
North Down	30,888	31.48	45.74	1.32	10.75	2.48	5.53	2.69
Omagh	16,123	37.96	33.62	0.42	14.58	1.17	8.45	3.80
Strabane	12,974	32.65	33.32	0.63	22.40	1.63	6.41	2.96
Health and Social Services Board								
Eastern	262,589	27.02	38.71	0.93	20.63	3.36	7.16	2.20
Northern	158,520	30.92	41.45	0.84	16.61	1.78	5.56	2.82
Southern	109,414	31.68	40.90	0.58	15.20	2.25	6.76	2.62
Western	96,195	30.60	36.46	0.56	20.10	2.44	6.93	2.90

Percentage of households:

Table KS18: Tenure (continued)

Area	All households	Owner occupied			Rented from[2]:			Other[3]
		Owns outright	Owns with a mortgage or loan	Shared ownership[1]	Northern Ireland Housing Executive	Housing Association, Housing Co-operative or Charitable Trust	Private landlord or letting agency	
Education and Library Board								
Belfast	**113,934**	24.05	31.02	1.01	26.35	4.74	11.04	1.78
North Eastern	**147,637**	30.33	41.86	0.84	16.89	1.83	5.46	2.78
South Eastern	**148,655**	29.30	44.60	0.87	16.24	2.30	4.18	2.51
Southern	**120,297**	32.34	40.46	0.60	14.99	2.15	6.78	2.68
Western	**96,195**	30.60	36.46	0.56	20.10	2.44	6.93	2.90
Parliamentary Constituency								
Belfast East	**34,824**	29.29	37.22	0.83	19.66	4.34	7.03	1.63
Belfast North	**36,383**	22.62	28.11	0.93	33.66	5.16	8.15	1.36
Belfast South	**39,715**	26.13	33.63	0.63	15.95	4.04	17.20	2.41
Belfast West	**30,992**	17.58	31.20	1.48	40.47	4.24	3.81	1.23
East Antrim	**32,789**	27.02	47.25	0.86	16.02	2.53	4.41	1.90
East Londonderry	**32,280**	30.77	37.74	1.06	17.35	1.68	7.90	3.51
Fermanagh and South Tyrone	**32,203**	39.69	33.93	0.38	14.01	1.46	7.27	3.26
Foyle	**35,947**	20.90	39.82	0.62	26.17	4.04	6.61	1.84
Lagan Valley	**38,405**	28.95	46.46	0.68	15.29	2.08	3.27	3.27
Mid Ulster	**28,350**	37.83	36.85	0.71	13.37	1.10	6.89	3.24
Newry and Armagh	**34,473**	33.33	39.83	0.49	15.59	1.36	6.89	2.52
North Antrim	**37,582**	34.63	37.50	0.67	17.40	1.56	5.48	2.76
North Down	**34,931**	31.64	44.74	1.31	11.64	2.50	5.53	2.64
South Antrim	**36,725**	27.45	48.64	0.88	14.23	1.58	3.68	3.54
South Down	**35,605**	34.69	40.24	0.62	12.46	1.57	7.13	3.28
Strangford	**37,898**	28.33	46.68	0.79	16.71	1.94	3.67	1.87
Upper Bann	**38,519**	25.49	43.31	0.80	17.75	3.99	6.46	2.20
West Tyrone	**29,097**	35.59	33.49	0.52	18.07	1.37	7.54	3.42
NUTS Level III								
Belfast	**113,934**	24.05	31.02	1.01	26.35	4.74	11.04	1.78
Outer Belfast	**143,724**	27.54	46.70	0.90	16.60	2.38	3.72	2.16
East of Northern Ireland	**147,875**	29.79	42.18	0.73	16.50	2.46	5.40	2.93
North of Northern Ireland	**96,724**	28.17	37.35	0.80	21.55	2.49	6.93	2.71
West and South of Northern Ireland	**124,461**	36.81	37.14	0.51	13.94	1.26	7.28	3.06

Percentage of households:

Notes:
1 Pays part rent and part mortgage.
2 Includes living in the household rent free.
3 Includes employer of a household member and relative or friend of a household member.

KS18

Table KS19: Rooms, Amenities, Central Heating and Lowest Floor Level

Area	All households	Average household size	Average number of rooms per household	With an occupancy rating of -1 or less[1]	With central heating and sole use of bath/shower and toilet	With central heating, without sole use of bath/shower and toilet	Without central heating, with sole use of bath/shower and toilet	Without central heating or sole use of bath/shower and toilet	Lowest floor level — Basement or semi-basement	Lowest floor level — Ground level (street level)	Lowest floor level — 1st/2nd/3rd or 4th floor	Lowest floor level — 5th floor or higher	Where all rooms are on one floor
Northern Ireland	**626,718**	**2.65**	**5.71**	**7.30**	**94.67**	**0.44**	**4.61**	**0.28**	**0.82**	**93.77**	**5.20**	**0.20**	**31.26**
Local Government District													
Antrim	17,178	2.71	5.89	5.44	95.51	0.30	3.91	0.28	0.49	95.31	4.19	-	28.01
Ards	28,689	2.53	5.72	5.14	94.61	0.32	4.82	0.25	1.09	94.73	4.17	-	33.05
Armagh	18,471	2.89	5.97	6.84	93.57	0.59	5.41	0.43	1.13	95.25	3.61	-	42.58
Ballymena	22,059	2.63	5.96	5.01	93.27	0.53	5.87	0.33	0.58	94.86	4.56	-	30.21
Ballymoney	9,635	2.77	5.92	7.36	92.77	0.40	6.55	0.28	0.53	96.61	2.86	-	44.26
Banbridge	15,188	2.71	5.98	6.02	94.19	0.37	5.16	0.28	1.13	94.84	4.03	-	36.72
Belfast	113,934	2.38	5.20	9.86	94.97	0.43	4.43	0.17	0.60	91.13	7.74	0.53	18.42
Carrickfergus	14,785	2.52	5.76	4.19	94.89	0.32	4.72	0.06	0.33	94.20	5.46	-	31.61
Castlereagh	26,887	2.44	5.66	3.30	97.69	0.33	1.95	0.03	1.07	92.09	6.22	0.62	22.67
Coleraine	21,583	2.56	5.96	5.63	94.63	0.44	4.83	0.11	0.57	93.94	5.49	0.01	40.58
Cookstown	10,883	2.97	6.02	8.23	92.31	0.63	6.54	0.51	1.36	95.05	3.59	-	41.35
Craigavon	30,182	2.65	5.66	6.58	95.95	0.38	3.40	0.27	0.41	95.08	4.50	0.01	31.34
Derry	35,947	2.87	5.54	11.40	96.40	0.50	2.97	0.13	0.97	93.45	5.54	0.04	26.29
Down	22,329	2.80	5.92	7.48	93.77	0.45	5.45	0.34	1.46	94.56	3.98	-	41.03
Dungannon	16,259	2.91	5.95	8.11	93.36	0.65	5.55	0.44	1.15	95.33	3.51	-	39.39
Fermanagh	20,454	2.78	5.95	7.84	91.30	0.60	7.13	0.97	0.88	95.09	4.03	0.01	44.21
Larne	12,250	2.50	5.80	4.29	92.37	0.39	6.87	0.38	1.33	92.18	5.53	0.96	28.82
Limavady	10,697	2.96	5.80	9.99	95.19	0.42	4.14	0.24	0.66	95.84	3.50	-	44.80
Lisburn	39,862	2.67	5.77	6.47	96.21	0.33	3.32	0.15	0.77	94.14	4.70	0.39	29.35
Magherafelt	12,957	3.05	6.00	9.44	92.45	0.48	6.52	0.55	0.93	95.73	3.34	-	42.00
Moyle	5,888	2.68	5.86	7.71	90.23	0.37	8.95	0.44	1.14	95.31	3.55	-	37.16
Newry and Mourne	29,314	2.94	5.82	9.14	93.65	0.69	5.15	0.51	0.98	95.23	3.77	0.02	38.49
Newtownabbey	31,302	2.51	5.69	4.44	96.54	0.29	3.10	0.08	0.38	92.67	6.28	0.67	28.72
North Down	30,888	2.41	5.92	3.53	95.92	0.37	3.63	0.08	1.29	92.43	6.27	0.01	26.48
Omagh	16,123	2.91	5.98	8.34	93.41	0.63	5.26	0.71	0.86	95.50	3.64	-	44.48
Strabane	12,974	2.94	5.66	11.26	91.14	0.50	7.76	0.60	0.62	95.92	3.45	-	41.81
Health and Social Services Board													
Eastern	262,589	2.49	5.54	7.21	95.41	0.39	4.04	0.17	0.88	92.52	6.24	0.35	24.98
Northern	158,520	2.65	5.87	5.72	94.15	0.40	5.19	0.25	0.66	94.29	4.84	0.21	33.95
Southern	109,414	2.82	5.84	7.46	94.30	0.54	4.77	0.39	0.89	95.15	3.94	0.01	37.10
Western	96,195	2.88	5.75	9.95	93.97	0.53	5.02	0.48	0.85	94.74	4.39	0.02	37.30

Percentage of households:

© Crown copyright 2002

KS19

Area	All households	Average household size	Average number of rooms per household	With an occupancy rating of -1 or less[1]	With central heating and sole use of bath/shower and toilet	With central heating, without sole use of bath/shower and toilet	Without central heating, with sole use of bath/shower and toilet	Without central heating or sole use of bath/shower and toilet	Lowest floor level — Basement or semi-basement	Ground level (street level)	1st/2nd/3rd or 4th floor	5th floor or higher	Where all rooms are on one floor
Education and Library Board													
Belfast	113,934	2.38	5.20	9.86	94.97	0.43	4.43	0.17	0.60	91.13	7.74	0.53	18.42
North Eastern	147,637	2.63	5.86	5.54	94.28	0.39	5.09	0.24	0.61	94.23	4.93	0.22	33.41
South Eastern	148,655	2.57	5.79	5.18	95.74	0.35	3.74	0.16	1.10	93.59	5.09	0.22	30.01
Southern	120,297	2.83	5.86	7.53	94.12	0.54	4.93	0.40	0.94	95.14	3.91	0.01	37.48
Western	96,195	2.88	5.75	9.95	93.97	0.53	5.02	0.48	0.85	94.74	4.39	0.02	37.30
Parliamentary Constituency													
Belfast East	34,824	2.25	5.41	5.34	95.49	0.34	4.04	0.13	0.74	91.61	7.08	0.57	17.81
Belfast North	36,383	2.34	5.08	9.63	94.38	0.44	5.06	0.12	0.66	89.61	8.50	1.23	21.23
Belfast South	39,715	2.29	5.42	7.10	95.33	0.40	4.10	0.17	0.72	89.18	9.59	0.52	20.88
Belfast West	30,992	2.80	4.99	16.33	96.32	0.51	3.03	0.15	0.51	92.92	6.16	0.41	18.93
East Antrim	32,789	2.52	5.82	4.15	94.39	0.34	5.10	0.17	0.70	93.59	5.35	0.36	29.10
East Londonderry	32,280	2.69	5.91	7.08	94.81	0.43	4.60	0.15	0.60	94.57	4.83	0.01	41.98
Fermanagh and South Tyrone	32,203	2.80	5.96	7.60	91.83	0.61	6.76	0.79	1.04	95.03	3.92	0.01	41.91
Foyle	35,947	2.87	5.54	11.40	96.40	0.50	2.97	0.13	0.97	93.45	5.54	0.04	26.29
Lagan Valley	38,405	2.59	5.90	4.34	95.86	0.31	3.66	0.17	0.81	94.60	4.20	0.39	30.52
Mid Ulster	28,350	3.03	5.99	9.14	92.79	0.57	6.14	0.50	1.05	95.57	3.37	-	41.95
Newry and Armagh	34,473	2.89	5.81	8.31	93.85	0.65	5.03	0.47	1.04	95.14	3.80	0.02	38.60
North Antrim	37,582	2.67	5.93	6.03	92.67	0.47	6.53	0.34	0.66	95.38	3.96	-	34.90
North Down	34,931	2.40	5.90	3.67	95.73	0.37	3.80	0.10	1.22	92.56	6.21	0.01	27.48
South Antrim	36,725	2.66	5.84	4.67	96.34	0.29	3.18	0.19	0.46	95.54	3.99	0.01	27.59
South Down	35,605	2.90	5.98	7.84	93.25	0.52	5.80	0.43	1.23	95.01	3.76	-	42.90
Strangford	37,898	2.57	5.75	4.80	95.32	0.33	4.14	0.21	1.19	94.56	4.24	0.01	31.58
Upper Bann	38,519	2.65	5.70	6.54	95.88	0.37	3.52	0.23	0.53	94.87	4.59	0.01	31.57
West Tyrone	29,097	2.92	5.83	9.64	92.39	0.57	6.38	0.66	0.75	95.69	3.56	-	43.29
NUTS Level III													
Belfast	113,934	2.38	5.20	9.86	94.97	0.43	4.43	0.17	0.60	91.13	7.74	0.53	18.42
Outer Belfast	143,724	2.52	5.76	4.57	96.36	0.33	3.22	0.09	0.81	93.07	5.75	0.37	27.58
East of Northern Ireland	147,875	2.65	5.83	5.82	94.43	0.39	4.88	0.29	0.89	94.66	4.37	0.08	32.92
North of Northern Ireland	96,724	2.80	5.74	9.31	94.43	0.46	4.88	0.23	0.77	94.58	4.64	0.02	36.06
West and South of Northern Ireland	124,461	2.91	5.94	8.30	92.94	0.62	5.85	0.59	1.02	95.29	3.68	0.01	41.55

Note:
1 The occupancy rating provides a measure of under-occupancy and overcrowding. For example, a value of -1 implies there is one room too few and that there is overcrowding in the household. The occupancy rating assumes that every household, including one person households, requires a minimum of two common rooms (excluding bathrooms).

Table KS20: Household Composition

Area	All households	One person		One family and no others					Cohabiting couple households			Lone parent households		Other households			
		Pensioner	Other	All pensioner	Married couple households			No children	With dependent children[1]	All children non-dependent	With dependent children[1]	All children non-dependent	With dependent children[1]	All student	All pensioner	Other
					No children	With dependent children[1]	All children non-dependent									
Northern Ireland	**626,718**	**12.84**	**14.53**	**6.51**	**10.61**	**24.29**	**8.04**	**2.12**	**1.58**	**0.17**	**8.08**	**4.63**	**2.51**	**0.28**	**0.69**	**3.14**
Local Government District																
Antrim	17,178	9.59	14.35	5.61	13.24	27.06	8.42	2.30	1.93	0.20	7.40	4.24	2.55	-	0.48	2.63
Ards	28,689	12.58	13.49	7.61	14.29	23.95	8.87	2.74	1.87	0.17	5.99	3.95	1.84	-	0.57	2.06
Armagh	18,471	12.43	11.55	5.76	10.29	30.26	9.61	1.29	1.10	0.12	6.42	5.05	2.69	-	0.82	2.61
Ballymena	22,060	12.20	12.69	7.41	13.07	24.52	9.15	1.94	1.65	0.16	6.57	4.78	2.37	0.01	0.90	2.59
Ballymoney	9,635	11.99	11.32	6.65	11.75	26.90	8.79	2.00	1.52	0.12	6.72	4.66	2.75	-	0.90	3.92
Banbridge	15,188	11.36	13.81	6.31	12.25	28.20	8.93	2.27	1.38	0.20	5.45	4.64	2.19	-	0.65	2.36
Belfast	113,934	15.82	19.51	6.31	7.56	15.22	6.10	2.52	1.58	0.16	11.02	4.97	2.58	1.04	0.70	4.91
Carrickfergus	14,785	12.00	14.33	7.41	13.43	23.96	7.60	3.00	2.21	0.25	7.76	3.65	1.97	0.04	0.34	2.05
Castlereagh	26,887	14.09	15.23	9.31	12.31	23.47	7.81	2.44	1.37	0.16	5.67	3.99	1.40	0.01	0.49	2.25
Coleraine	21,583	13.02	14.06	7.54	12.05	22.79	7.03	2.20	1.92	0.16	7.43	3.92	2.49	1.65	0.66	3.07
Cookstown	10,883	11.68	11.23	5.51	9.87	31.10	9.36	1.19	1.16	0.15	6.65	5.15	2.83	0.07	0.89	3.14
Craigavon	30,184	12.62	14.75	6.29	10.86	25.52	8.14	1.87	1.86	0.14	8.08	4.39	2.39	0.01	0.61	2.47
Derry	35,947	9.54	14.79	4.29	7.96	25.71	7.76	1.93	1.53	0.16	12.70	4.99	4.08	0.23	0.63	3.72
Down	22,329	11.91	12.52	6.38	10.74	27.96	8.49	1.84	1.75	0.19	7.32	4.76	2.75	-	0.77	2.62
Dungannon	16,259	12.36	12.47	5.69	9.57	29.65	9.30	1.22	0.89	0.18	6.91	5.28	2.69	-	0.92	2.89
Fermanagh	20,454	13.41	13.15	5.51	9.85	27.84	8.60	1.44	1.34	0.14	6.26	5.04	2.55	0.05	1.05	3.78
Larne	12,250	13.40	14.91	7.27	12.72	22.64	8.06	2.88	1.91	0.13	6.47	4.54	2.10	-	0.75	2.23
Limavady	10,697	9.33	10.65	4.68	10.89	30.67	9.00	1.92	2.07	0.22	7.30	5.54	3.45	0.09	0.75	3.43
Lisburn	39,862	11.28	13.66	6.73	12.04	25.55	8.27	2.40	1.78	0.18	8.83	4.26	2.44	0.01	0.49	2.07
Magherafelt	12,956	11.28	10.04	5.06	9.20	31.86	10.22	1.30	1.33	0.14	6.00	5.40	3.06	-	0.98	4.14
Moyle	5,888	13.91	14.40	5.94	10.70	24.42	8.10	0.99	1.32	0.14	7.57	5.26	2.67	-	1.29	3.28
Newry and Mourne	29,314	12.33	12.34	5.14	8.58	30.63	9.14	1.22	1.09	0.12	7.73	4.94	2.88	0.03	0.85	2.96
Newtownabbey	31,302	12.75	13.99	8.21	12.79	23.29	8.66	2.82	1.62	0.22	7.30	4.02	1.79	0.14	0.41	1.99
North Down	30,888	15.02	14.47	8.96	13.67	22.52	7.40	2.81	1.75	0.21	5.53	3.58	1.52	0.02	0.52	2.03
Omagh	16,123	11.75	13.19	4.98	8.84	30.73	8.37	1.03	1.19	0.09	7.58	5.36	2.72	0.02	0.84	3.31
Strabane	12,975	11.49	11.58	5.17	8.72	27.99	9.23	1.09	1.39	0.18	8.83	5.33	3.85	0.02	0.83	4.28
Health and Social Services Board																
Eastern	262,589	14.17	16.34	7.14	10.45	20.53	7.26	2.50	1.66	0.17	8.63	4.47	2.24	0.46	0.62	3.36
Northern	158,520	12.15	13.30	6.96	12.20	25.31	8.50	2.22	1.70	0.18	7.03	4.42	2.36	0.26	0.68	2.73
Southern	109,414	12.30	13.10	5.81	10.16	28.68	8.94	1.56	1.31	0.15	7.16	4.82	2.59	0.01	0.76	2.67
Western	96,195	10.97	13.28	4.83	8.94	27.86	8.38	1.56	1.48	0.15	9.35	5.17	3.42	0.11	0.79	3.71

Table KS20: Household Composition (continued)

Area	All households	One family and no others			Married couple households			Cohabiting couple households			Lone parent households		Other households			
		One person		All pensioner	No children	With dependent children[1]	All children non-dependent	No children	With dependent children[1]	All children non-dependent	With dependent children[1]	All children non-dependent	With dependent children[1]	All student	All pensioner	Other
		Pensioner	Other													
Education and Library Board																
Belfast	113,934	15.82	19.51	6.31	7.56	15.22	6.10	2.52	1.58	0.16	11.02	4.97	2.58	1.04	0.70	4.91
North Eastern	147,637	12.19	13.45	7.06	12.37	24.89	8.43	2.30	1.74	0.18	7.06	4.36	2.32	0.28	0.67	2.70
South Eastern	148,655	12.91	13.91	7.78	12.67	24.60	8.16	2.47	1.71	0.18	6.80	4.09	1.99	0.01	0.55	2.17
Southern	120,297	12.24	12.93	5.78	10.13	28.90	8.98	1.52	1.30	0.15	7.12	4.85	2.61	0.02	0.77	2.72
Western	96,195	10.97	13.28	4.83	8.94	27.86	8.38	1.56	1.48	0.15	9.35	5.17	3.42	0.11	0.79	3.71
Parliamentary Constituency																
Belfast East	34,824	17.71	18.30	8.86	10.30	17.12	6.41	2.60	1.42	0.21	7.43	4.55	1.53	0.03	0.64	2.88
Belfast North	36,383	17.85	18.59	6.82	7.29	14.59	6.35	2.04	1.75	0.15	13.28	5.29	2.55	0.09	0.65	2.71
Belfast South	39,715	14.04	23.19	6.37	8.11	15.42	5.21	3.56	1.20	0.11	6.25	3.37	1.38	2.87	0.57	8.35
Belfast West	30,992	12.38	14.29	4.74	5.72	17.54	7.71	1.38	1.98	0.18	18.28	6.84	5.06	0.07	0.72	3.10
East Antrim	32,789	12.33	14.43	7.48	13.31	23.91	7.79	2.98	2.04	0.18	7.02	3.91	1.93	0.10	0.48	2.10
East Londonderry	32,280	11.80	12.93	6.60	11.67	25.40	7.68	2.11	1.97	0.18	7.39	4.46	2.81	1.13	0.69	3.19
Fermanagh and South Tyrone	32,203	13.31	13.04	5.75	9.94	28.08	8.80	1.40	1.14	0.16	6.25	5.11	2.56	0.03	1.02	3.42
Foyle	35,947	9.54	14.79	4.29	7.96	25.71	7.76	1.93	1.53	0.16	12.70	4.99	4.08	0.23	0.63	3.72
Lagan Valley	38,405	11.89	13.91	7.25	13.34	26.29	8.41	2.57	1.65	0.18	5.93	4.00	1.92	0.01	0.55	2.11
Mid Ulster	28,350	11.29	10.73	5.13	9.29	31.69	9.81	1.20	1.23	0.14	6.67	5.31	2.96	0.03	0.91	3.59
Newry and Armagh	34,473	12.55	12.51	5.22	9.03	29.32	9.28	1.29	1.09	0.12	7.70	5.40	2.87	0.03	0.79	2.81
North Antrim	37,583	12.41	12.61	6.98	12.36	25.12	8.89	1.81	1.56	0.15	6.76	4.82	2.51	0.01	0.96	3.04
North Down	34,931	15.24	14.51	9.06	13.80	22.14	7.33	2.75	1.76	0.19	5.52	3.63	1.53	0.02	0.54	1.98
South Antrim	36,725	10.37	13.17	6.80	13.60	26.50	9.08	2.59	1.73	0.22	6.94	4.10	2.21	-	0.48	2.22
South Down	35,605	11.98	11.81	6.13	10.09	30.18	9.15	1.49	1.45	0.16	6.72	4.49	2.72	-	0.88	2.76
Strangford	37,898	12.00	13.28	7.44	13.97	25.44	8.84	2.68	1.82	0.18	5.93	3.96	1.84	-	0.54	2.07
Upper Bann	38,518	12.36	14.76	6.30	11.11	25.97	8.13	2.00	1.77	0.17	7.69	4.45	2.30	-	0.58	2.41
West Tyrone	29,097	11.63	12.47	5.07	8.79	29.51	8.75	1.06	1.28	0.13	8.14	5.35	3.23	0.02	0.84	3.74
NUTS Level III																
Belfast	113,934	15.82	19.51	6.31	7.56	15.22	6.10	2.52	1.58	0.16	11.02	4.97	2.58	1.04	0.70	4.91
Outer Belfast	143,724	13.00	14.27	8.09	12.75	23.86	8.01	2.65	1.71	0.20	7.08	3.95	1.86	0.04	0.46	2.08
East of Northern Ireland	147,875	12.03	13.73	6.73	12.41	25.65	8.59	2.22	1.78	0.17	6.85	4.44	2.31	0.00	0.67	2.42
North of Northern Ireland	96,724	11.06	13.37	5.51	9.84	25.95	8.05	1.83	1.64	0.17	9.50	4.84	3.41	0.47	0.74	3.61
West and South of Northern Ireland	124,461	12.28	12.15	5.37	9.38	30.17	9.17	1.25	1.15	0.13	6.89	5.14	2.77	0.03	0.90	3.22

Note:
1 A dependent child is a person in a household aged 0-15 (whether or not in a family) or a person aged 16-18 who is a full-time student and in a family with parent(s).

KS20

Table KS21: Households with Dependent Children and Households with Limiting Long-term Illness

Area	All households	Percentage of households:				With one or more persons with a limiting long-term illness
		With no adults in employment:		With dependent children:		
		With dependent children[1]	Without dependent children[1]	All ages	Aged 0-4	
Northern Ireland	**626,718**	**7.25**	**29.83**	**36.47**	**14.35**	**41.31**
Local Government District						
Antrim	17,178	5.16	23.47	38.94	16.33	36.03
Ards	28,689	4.37	28.73	33.66	12.97	38.30
Armagh	18,471	6.45	27.07	40.47	16.44	41.76
Ballymena	22,059	4.88	27.76	35.11	13.42	35.83
Ballymoney	9,635	5.88	28.30	37.89	15.35	41.55
Banbridge	15,188	4.38	25.53	37.21	15.07	38.52
Belfast	113,934	9.65	36.32	30.40	11.69	44.89
Carrickfergus	14,785	4.87	27.70	35.91	13.40	36.73
Castlereagh	26,887	3.75	30.37	31.91	12.79	36.43
Coleraine	21,583	6.47	30.70	34.63	13.20	36.73
Cookstown	10,883	8.11	27.95	41.75	16.58	48.73
Craigavon	30,182	7.19	29.85	37.86	14.77	44.08
Derry	35,947	13.41	28.35	44.02	17.76	46.06
Down	22,329	6.25	27.28	39.81	15.34	39.92
Dungannon	16,259	8.06	28.58	40.14	16.51	45.97
Fermanagh	20,454	6.88	29.25	38.00	14.55	40.61
Larne	12,250	4.68	31.06	33.13	12.28	37.40
Limavady	10,697	8.11	24.48	43.50	17.86	42.61
Lisburn	39,862	7.05	25.73	38.61	15.37	37.92
Magherafelt	12,957	6.30	24.40	42.25	17.60	42.58
Moyle	5,888	7.98	33.29	35.99	14.16	43.94
Newry and Mourne	29,314	9.49	29.25	42.34	17.49	45.78
Newtownabbey	31,302	4.94	29.25	34.00	13.26	37.58
North Down	30,888	3.44	31.82	31.32	11.05	34.65
Omagh	16,123	8.47	28.08	42.24	16.71	45.03
Strabane	12,974	10.74	29.71	42.08	17.81	50.84
Health and Social Services Board						
Eastern	262,589	7.05	31.98	33.07	12.73	40.62
Northern	158,520	5.64	28.21	36.41	14.29	38.61
Southern	109,414	7.42	28.43	39.75	16.08	43.65
Western	96,195	10.24	28.25	42.12	16.92	44.99

Table KS21: Households with Dependent Children and Households with Limiting Long-term Illness (continued)

Area	All households	With no adults in employment:		With dependent children¹: Percentage of households:		With one or more persons with a limiting long-term illness
		With dependent children¹	Without dependent children¹	All ages	Aged 0-4	
Education and Library Board						
Belfast	**113,934**	9.65	36.32	30.40	11.69	44.89
North Eastern	**147,637**	5.45	28.23	36.01	14.12	37.87
South Eastern	**148,655**	5.07	28.65	35.11	13.54	37.35
Southern	**120,297**	7.48	28.39	39.93	16.13	44.11
Western	**96,195**	10.24	28.25	42.12	16.92	44.99
Parliamentary Constituency						
Belfast East	**34,824**	5.57	36.73	27.50	10.33	40.60
Belfast North	**36,383**	11.53	40.65	32.17	12.25	50.18
Belfast South	**39,715**	4.88	31.56	24.26	9.71	33.59
Belfast West	**30,992**	17.55	33.77	42.86	16.86	55.43
East Antrim	**32,789**	4.69	28.82	34.90	13.19	36.55
East Londonderry	**32,280**	7.01	28.64	37.57	14.74	38.68
Fermanagh and South Tyrone	**32,203**	6.71	29.32	38.03	14.85	42.07
Foyle	**35,947**	13.41	28.35	44.02	17.76	46.06
Lagan Valley	**38,405**	4.10	25.80	35.79	14.39	35.59
Mid Ulster	**28,350**	7.96	26.07	42.57	17.51	46.04
Newry and Armagh	**34,473**	8.93	29.14	40.99	16.76	44.84
North Antrim	**37,582**	5.63	28.76	35.96	14.03	38.57
North Down	**34,931**	3.50	32.31	30.94	10.89	35.29
South Antrim	**36,725**	4.61	24.57	37.38	15.06	35.65
South Down	**35,605**	6.44	27.02	41.09	16.30	41.40
Strangford	**37,898**	4.18	27.40	35.04	13.72	37.29
Upper Bann	**38,519**	6.66	29.11	37.73	14.78	43.07
West Tyrone	**29,097**	9.48	28.81	42.17	17.20	47.62
NUTS Level III						
Belfast	**113,934**	9.65	36.32	30.40	11.69	44.89
Outer Belfast	**143,724**	4.97	28.88	34.51	13.30	36.74
East of Northern Ireland	**147,875**	5.42	27.85	36.60	14.31	39.04
North of Northern Ireland	**96,724**	9.84	28.92	40.51	16.30	43.66
West and South of Northern Ireland	**124,461**	7.84	28.07	40.99	16.56	44.19

Note:
1   A dependent child is a person in a household aged 0-15 (whether or not in a family) or a person aged 16-18 who is a full time student in a family with parent(s).

K S 2 1

Table KS22: Lone Parent Households with Dependent Children

Area	All lone parent households with dependent children[1]	Male lone parent with dependent children[1]			Female lone parent with dependent children[1]		
		Total	Percentage in full-time[2] employment	Percentage in part-time[2] employment	Total	Percentage in full-time[2] employment	Percentage in part-time[2] employment
Northern Ireland	**50,641**	**3,928**	**45.24**	**6.82**	**46,713**	**17.49**	**23.93**
Local Government District							
Antrim	1,270	90	58.89	8.89	1,180	22.37	24.07
Ards	1,720	163	46.01	14.11	1,557	23.83	23.13
Armagh	1,183	98	45.92	9.18	1,085	18.34	21.84
Ballymena	1,449	128	62.50	3.91	1,321	20.21	25.44
Ballymoney	648	51	52.94	5.88	597	20.77	20.94
Banbridge	827	107	52.34	6.54	720	22.08	23.19
Belfast	12,560	735	34.42	5.17	11,825	12.55	23.74
Carrickfergus	1,148	143	55.94	2.10	1,005	28.76	24.18
Castlereagh	1,524	125	62.40	10.40	1,399	26.09	25.45
Coleraine	1,604	126	52.38	9.52	1,478	19.89	22.87
Cookstown	722	57	42.11	8.77	665	15.49	23.00
Craigavon	2,438	179	36.87	6.70	2,259	19.12	21.74
Derry	4,563	301	31.89	6.31	4,262	12.41	14.29
Down	1,637	132	50.76	6.06	1,505	22.46	21.73
Dungannon	1,123	96	52.08	3.13	1,027	13.73	17.53
Fermanagh	1,281	142	52.82	9.15	1,139	17.91	13.88
Larne	795	83	51.81	4.82	712	23.03	25.97
Limavady	780	59	55.93	-	721	19.97	15.64
Lisburn	3,518	259	43.24	6.18	3,259	18.17	22.58
Magherafelt	776	76	60.53	6.58	700	21.00	15.00
Moyle	445	41	51.22	7.32	404	12.87	13.83
Newry and Mourne	2,265	186	37.10	11.29	2,079	12.65	13.88
Newtownabbey	2,284	192	47.92	5.21	2,092	24.33	23.85
North Down	1,706	160	66.25	7.50	1,546	26.52	28.20
Omagh	1,224	110	34.55	5.45	1,114	17.32	13.25
Strabane	1,146	83	31.33	12.05	1,063	12.51	13.45
Health and Social Services Board							
Eastern	22,663	1,573	43.93	6.99	21,090	16.88	22.57
Northern	11,145	990	53.74	5.66	10,155	21.79	22.88
Southern	7,839	669	42.75	7.77	7,170	16.65	19.89
Western	8,992	694	38.62	7.20	8,298	14.50	15.28

Table KS22: Lone Parent Households with Dependent Children (continued)

Area	All lone parent households with dependent children[1]	Male lone parent with dependent children[1]			Female lone parent with dependent children[1]		
		Total	Percentage in full-time[2] employment	Percentage in part-time[2] employment	Total	Percentage in full-time[2] employment	Percentage in part-time[2] employment
Education and Library Board							
Belfast	12,560	735	34.42	5.17	11,825	12.55	20.74
North Eastern	10,421	932	54.51	5.47	9,489	22.24	23.08
South Eastern	10,101	836	52.39	8.61	9,265	22.41	24.90
Southern	8,563	727	42.64	7.84	7,836	16.55	19.90
Western	8,995	697	38.45	7.17	8,298	14.50	15.28
Parliamentary Constituency							
Belfast East	2,587	202	42.57	9.41	2,385	18.74	23.69
Belfast North	4,831	274	29.56	3.28	4,557	11.43	20.43
Belfast South	2,481	152	46.05	4.61	2,329	18.98	21.98
Belfast West	5,664	295	27.12	6.10	5,369	9.24	18.94
East Antrim	2,302	251	54.58	3.59	2,051	26.47	24.62
East Londonderry	2,385	187	52.94	7.49	2,198	19.93	20.84
Fermanagh and South Tyrone	2,013	207	56.04	6.76	1,806	17.11	19.66
Foyle	4,563	301	31.89	6.31	4,262	12.41	14.29
Lagan Valley	2,278	211	50.24	4.74	2,067	25.50	26.71
Mid Ulster	1,892	166	47.59	7.23	1,726	16.57	16.11
Newry and Armagh	2,654	207	37.20	8.70	2,447	14.43	18.10
North Antrim	2,542	219	58.45	4.57	2,323	19.07	22.77
North Down	1,928	183	63.93	7.10	1,745	25.90	28.37
South Antrim	2,551	207	56.52	6.76	2,344	25.21	24.45
South Down	2,391	209	47.85	10.53	2,182	19.48	20.99
Strangford	2,246	215	56.28	12.56	2,031	25.26	27.97
Upper Bann	2,963	248	41.53	6.85	2,715	19.48	22.25
West Tyrone	2,367	190	33.68	8.42	2,177	14.97	14.88
NUTS Level III							
Belfast	12,560	735	34.42	5.17	11,825	12.55	20.74
Outer Belfast	10,182	881	53.12	6.02	9,301	23.28	24.56
East of Northern Ireland	10,133	881	49.94	7.60	9,252	21.56	24.16
North of Northern Ireland	9,187	662	40.63	7.25	8,525	14.97	16.46
West and South of Northern Ireland	8,578	768	45.18	8.07	7,810	16.01	17.95

Notes:
1 A dependent child is a person in a household aged 0-15 (whether or not in a family) or a person aged 16-18 who is a full time student in a family with parent(s).
2 For the Census, part-time is defined as working 30 hours or less a week. Full-time is defined as working 31 or more hours a week.

KS22

Table KS23: Communal Establishment Residents[1]

Area	All communal establishments	Number of communal establishment residents[1]	Percentage of communal establishment residents living in:								Percentage of communal establishments residents with a limiting long term illness living in:	
			Medical and care establishments:						Education establishments	Other establishments	Medical and care establishments	Other establishments (including education establishments)
			'NHS/HSSB' managed[2]:			Non 'NHS/HSSB' managed[2]:						
			Psychiatric, General or other hospital or home	Residential care home	Children's, Nursing or other medical and care home	Nursing home	Residential care home	Other				
Northern Ireland	**1,027**	**24,257**	**6.72**	**5.72**	**0.94**	**27.98**	**12.52**	**2.07**	**17.05**	**27.00**	**90.44**	**9.56**
Local Government District												
Antrim	28	1,617	28.39	1.67	3.09	6.43	4.39	2.91	-	53.12	95.90	4.10
Ards	39	543	-	18.42	-	57.83	19.52	1.47	-	2.76	98.03	1.97
Armagh	43	951	26.50	-	-	35.86	10.41	-	6.52	20.72	96.71	3.29
Ballymena	32	573	2.79	5.58	1.75	45.90	17.63	10.99	-	15.36	89.40	10.60
Ballymoney	15	109	-	24.77	-	2.75	72.48	-	-	-	100.00	-
Banbridge	16	219	-	24.66	1.37	63.47	6.39	-	2.28	1.83	100.00	-
Belfast	233	5,499	3.49	3.40	0.40	18.91	13.77	1.07	48.12	10.84	82.66	17.34
Carrickfergus	17	330	-	21.21	6.36	40.91	10.30	-	-	21.21	83.17	16.83
Castlereagh	34	816	28.55	7.35	-	35.54	14.46	5.27	-	8.82	94.95	5.05
Coleraine	43	1,024	-	0.29	-	26.76	22.56	-	40.43	9.96	86.96	13.04
Cookstown	14	285	-	9.82	-	60.35	-	-	24.56	5.26	96.59	3.41
Craigavon	25	521	4.80	0.58	1.15	62.38	12.28	1.97	-	18.81	94.62	5.38
Derry	62	1,672	8.07	5.08	1.20	19.68	9.63	-	13.28	41.09	82.32	17.68
Down	60	1,218	8.87	7.96	0.66	30.71	17.90	-	-	33.91	94.16	5.84
Dungannon	29	399	0.75	8.77	10.28	57.89	5.26	1.00	9.77	6.27	97.83	2.17
Fermanagh	46	533	4.69	11.07	-	53.66	23.26	0.56	2.06	4.69	98.32	1.68
Larne	19	201	1.99	23.88	-	23.38	35.82	3.98	-	10.95	94.89	5.11
Limavady	10	749	-	3.60	-	12.55	2.00	1.74	-	80.11	59.84	40.16
Lisburn	42	1,976	2.28	4.81	-	23.73	4.20	2.33	0.15	62.50	83.09	16.91
Magherafelt	18	123	2.44	9.76	2.44	32.52	47.15	2.44	-	3.25	97.37	2.63
Moyle	19	145	-	26.90	-	46.90	19.31	-	-	6.90	97.69	2.31
Newry and Mourne	53	616	2.44	12.01	3.25	35.06	21.59	7.47	-	18.18	89.77	10.23
Newtownabbey	29	1,283	0.47	7.09	0.78	36.87	1.48	0.86	51.68	0.78	96.20	3.80
North Down	57	1,757	-	4.21	0.68	30.05	17.36	6.49	-	41.21	95.32	4.68
Omagh	33	935	11.87	3.42	0.43	10.80	13.58	-	-	59.89	91.54	8.46
Strabane	11	167	-	17.37	-	78.44	-	-	-	4.19	100.00	-
Health and Social Services Board												
Eastern	465	11,807	4.90	5.19	0.36	25.54	13.44	2.29	22.42	25.87	88.99	11.01
Northern	234	5,686	8.55	6.61	1.64	27.77	12.19	2.32	20.17	20.75	92.69	7.31
Southern	166	2,708	10.89	6.13	2.58	46.23	12.22	1.85	3.99	16.10	95.23	4.77
Western	162	4,056	6.68	5.72	0.59	23.20	10.53	1.21	5.74	46.33	86.19	13.81

Table KS23: Communal Establishment Residents[1] (continued)

Area	All communal establishments	Number of communal establishment residents[1]	Medical and care establishments: 'NHS/HSSB' managed[2]: Psychiatric, General or other hospital or home	Residential care home	Children's, Nursing or other medical and care home	Non 'NHS/HSSB' managed[2]: Nursing home	Residential care home	Other	Education establishments	Other establishments	Percentage of communal establishments residents with a limiting long term illness living in: Medical and care establishments	Other establishments (including education establishments)
Education and Library Board												
Belfast	233	5,499	3.49	3.40	0.40	18.91	13.77	1.07	48.12	10.84	82.66	17.34
North Eastern	220	5,401	9.00	6.44	1.72	26.05	12.83	2.44	19.94	21.57	92.50	7.50
South Eastern	232	6,307	6.12	6.75	0.32	31.31	13.16	3.35	-	38.99	92.77	7.23
Southern	180	2,993	9.86	6.48	2.34	47.58	11.06	1.67	5.95	15.07	95.26	4.74
Western	162	4,056	6.68	5.72	0.59	23.20	10.53	1.21	5.74	46.33	86.19	13.81
Parliamentary Constituency												
Belfast East	42	873	-	8.02	-	45.93	37.80	0.80	6.30	1.15	99.45	0.55
Belfast North	57	917	1.53	5.13	1.74	56.27	10.47	1.20	0.98	22.68	86.63	13.37
Belfast South	130	3,897	5.36	2.08	0.15	9.78	6.70	1.33	66.26	8.34	76.72	23.28
Belfast West	32	650	25.54	9.85	-	27.85	18.00	-	-	18.77	86.97	13.03
East Antrim	44	1,313	0.30	12.03	2.36	19.12	8.07	0.61	50.50	7.01	86.41	13.59
East Londonderry	53	1,772	-	1.64	-	20.77	13.88	0.73	23.36	39.62	78.37	21.63
Fermanagh and South Tyrone	70	867	3.23	10.15	4.73	54.44	15.11	0.81	5.77	5.77	97.96	2.04
Foyle	62	1,672	8.07	5.08	1.20	19.68	9.63	1.97	13.28	41.09	82.32	17.68
Lagan Valley	43	2,006	2.24	5.78	-	24.08	4.14	2.29	-	61.47	84.02	15.98
Mid Ulster	37	467	-	9.85	-	55.03	15.42	0.64	14.99	4.07	96.88	3.12
Newry and Armagh	77	1,276	20.92	3.68	0.31	35.03	8.78	3.61	5.02	22.65	92.86	7.14
North Antrim	66	827	1.93	11.85	1.21	40.39	25.15	7.62	-	11.85	92.36	7.64
North Down	66	1,914	-	5.80	0.63	32.13	16.93	6.32	-	38.19	95.61	4.39
South Antrim	43	1,889	24.30	2.12	2.65	17.68	4.76	2.49	-	46.00	96.91	3.09
South Down	76	1,447	7.46	8.57	1.66	31.86	20.25	-	-	30.20	94.72	5.28
Strangford	50	741	5.67	12.55	-	46.69	27.40	5.94	-	1.75	98.68	1.32
Upper Bann	35	623	4.01	4.65	1.44	60.83	12.52	-	0.80	15.73	95.61	4.39
West Tyrone	44	1,102	10.07	5.54	0.36	21.05	11.52	-	-	51.45	93.90	6.10
NUTS Level III												
Belfast	233	5,499	3.49	3.40	0.40	18.91	13.77	1.07	48.12	10.84	82.66	17.34
Outer Belfast	179	6,160	4.61	6.33	0.70	30.76	9.07	3.47	10.78	34.27	91.40	8.60
East of Northern Ireland	219	4,892	12.51	7.38	1.57	32.01	13.21	2.58	0.10	30.64	94.88	5.12
North of Northern Ireland	160	3,865	3.49	5.41	0.52	23.26	13.30	1.19	16.46	36.38	83.99	16.01
West and South of Northern Ireland	236	3,841	10.60	6.25	1.74	36.11	14.63	1.46	4.79	24.42	95.09	4.91

Notes:
1 'Residents' excludes staff and families of staff.
2 'NHS/HSSB' refers to the Health and Personal Social Services in Northern Ireland.

KS23

Table KS24: Knowledge of Irish

Area	All persons aged 3 and over	Percentage of persons aged 3 and over who:						
		Understand spoken Irish but cannot read, write or speak Irish [1]	Speak but do not read or write Irish [1]	Speak and read but do not write Irish [1]	Speak, read, write and understand Irish	Have other combination of skills	Have some knowledge of Irish	Have no knowledge of Irish
Northern Ireland	**1,617,957**	2.25	1.52	0.44	4.64	1.49	10.35	89.65
Local Government District								
Antrim	**46,220**	1.72	1.13	0.41	3.53	1.08	7.87	92.13
Ards	**70,517**	0.75	0.40	0.12	1.25	0.49	3.02	96.98
Armagh	**51,875**	3.29	2.07	0.62	6.57	2.16	14.72	85.28
Ballymena	**56,422**	1.23	0.75	0.19	2.11	0.71	4.99	95.01
Ballymoney	**25,759**	1.52	1.05	0.28	3.05	1.13	7.03	92.97
Banbridge	**39,643**	1.43	0.80	0.24	2.73	0.95	6.15	93.85
Belfast	**267,716**	2.78	2.05	0.60	6.59	1.55	13.57	86.43
Carrickfergus	**36,231**	0.53	0.31	0.10	0.72	0.28	1.95	98.05
Castlereagh	**63,951**	0.96	0.61	0.23	1.86	0.63	4.28	95.72
Coleraine	**54,135**	1.25	0.87	0.19	3.01	0.93	6.26	93.74
Cookstown	**31,203**	3.37	1.98	0.54	5.85	2.68	14.41	85.59
Craigavon	**77,358**	2.12	1.57	0.47	4.67	1.60	10.44	89.56
Derry	**100,423**	2.86	1.75	0.59	6.43	2.12	13.75	86.25
Down	**61,272**	2.48	1.60	0.38	3.93	1.40	9.79	90.21
Dungannon	**45,598**	3.78	2.76	0.76	8.93	2.87	19.10	80.90
Fermanagh	**55,215**	2.84	1.69	0.58	5.42	2.35	12.88	87.12
Larne	**29,719**	1.00	0.76	0.21	1.63	0.80	4.40	95.60
Limavady	**30,972**	2.45	1.70	0.44	4.32	1.94	10.84	89.16
Lisburn	**104,163**	1.94	1.34	0.33	3.38	0.85	7.84	92.16
Magherafelt	**37,996**	3.77	2.79	0.72	7.72	2.54	17.54	82.46
Moyle	**15,279**	3.46	1.96	0.62	6.16	2.18	14.37	85.63
Newry and Mourne	**83,130**	4.30	2.95	0.91	9.08	3.17	20.41	79.59
Newtownabbey	**77,043**	0.92	0.63	0.19	1.95	0.65	4.33	95.67
North Down	**73,802**	0.74	0.35	0.14	1.01	0.44	2.67	97.33
Omagh	**45,811**	3.69	2.39	0.70	6.95	2.46	16.19	83.81
Strabane	**36,504**	2.61	1.64	0.43	5.13	1.95	11.76	88.24
Health and Social Services Board								
Eastern	**641,421**	1.97	1.37	0.39	4.11	1.09	8.94	91.06
Northern	**410,007**	1.65	1.09	0.31	3.22	1.14	7.40	92.60
Southern	**297,604**	3.10	2.13	0.63	6.63	2.25	14.73	85.27
Western	**268,925**	2.92	1.83	0.57	5.89	2.18	13.38	86.62

Area	All persons aged 3 and over	Percentage of persons aged 3 and over who:						
		Understand spoken Irish but cannot read, write or speak Irish	Speak but do not read or write Irish[1]	Speak and read but do not write Irish[1]	Speak, read, write and understand Irish	Have other combination of skills	Have some knowledge of Irish	Have no knowledge of Irish
Education and Library Board								
Belfast	267,716	2.78	2.05	0.60	6.59	1.55	13.57	86.43
North Eastern	378,804	1.51	1.02	0.29	3.00	1.01	6.83	93.17
South Eastern	373,705	1.40	0.89	0.24	2.34	0.75	5.62	94.38
Southern	328,807	3.12	2.11	0.62	6.55	2.29	14.70	85.30
Western	268,925	2.92	1.83	0.57	5.89	2.18	13.38	86.62
Parliamentary Constituency								
Belfast East	76,590	0.75	0.44	0.13	1.24	0.49	3.06	96.94
Belfast North	82,886	2.28	1.64	0.49	5.16	1.34	10.91	89.09
Belfast South	92,071	2.19	1.52	0.59	6.59	1.66	12.55	87.45
Belfast West	83,921	5.21	4.16	0.99	11.02	2.23	23.61	76.39
East Antrim	80,882	0.75	0.52	0.17	1.32	0.56	3.31	96.69
East Londonderry	85,107	1.69	1.17	0.28	3.49	1.30	7.92	92.08
Fermanagh and South Tyrone	87,379	2.93	1.84	0.58	6.11	2.36	13.82	86.18
Foyle	100,423	2.86	1.75	0.59	6.43	2.12	13.75	86.25
Lagan Valley	97,542	1.21	0.70	0.20	1.77	0.53	4.41	95.59
Mid Ulster	82,633	3.89	2.74	0.73	7.85	2.84	18.04	81.96
Newry and Armagh	96,453	4.04	2.59	0.78	8.22	2.77	18.41	81.59
North Antrim	97,460	1.66	1.02	0.28	2.99	1.05	7.00	93.00
North Down	83,189	0.72	0.34	0.13	0.97	0.44	2.60	97.40
South Antrim	95,755	1.35	0.89	0.30	2.74	0.88	6.16	93.84
South Down	100,279	2.98	2.09	0.57	5.58	1.98	13.21	86.79
Strangford	94,345	0.82	0.46	0.15	1.41	0.50	3.33	96.67
Upper Bann	98,727	1.98	1.39	0.42	4.32	1.50	9.61	90.39
West Tyrone	82,315	3.21	2.06	0.58	6.14	2.23	14.22	85.78
NUTS Level III								
Belfast	267,716	2.78	2.05	0.60	6.59	1.55	13.57	86.43
Outer Belfast	355,190	1.15	0.74	0.22	2.03	0.62	4.76	95.24
East of Northern Ireland	381,151	1.58	1.04	0.30	2.96	1.04	6.93	93.07
North of Northern Ireland	263,072	2.35	1.49	0.44	4.95	1.73	10.97	89.03
West and South of Northern Ireland	350,828	3.63	2.42	0.72	7.40	2.65	16.82	83.18

Note:
1 An ability to speak, read or write Irish does not imply an ability to understand spoken Irish unless stated. Persons in these categories may or may not have the ability to understand Irish.

KS24

Maps

Northern Ireland: Local Government Districts

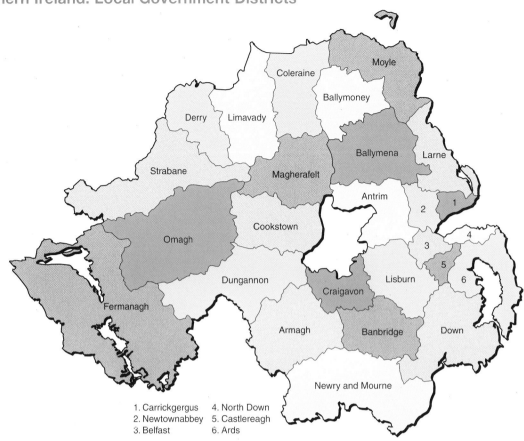

1. Carrickgergus
2. Newtownabbey
3. Belfast
4. North Down
5. Castlereagh
6. Ards

Northern Ireland: Health and Social Services Boards

Northern Ireland: Education and Library Boards

Northern Ireland: NUTS Level III

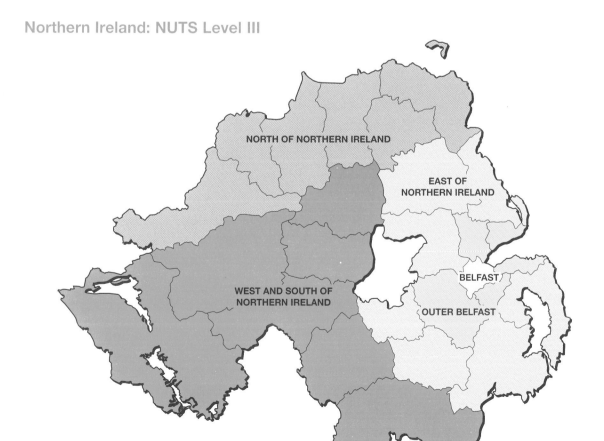

Northern Ireland: Parliamentary Constituencies

East Londonderry

Foyle

North Antrim

East Antrim

West Tyrone

Mid Ulster

South Antrim

1

2

4

3

Fermanagh and South Tyrone

Upper Bann

Lagan Valley

5

6

Newry and Armagh

South Down

1. Belfast North   4. Belfast East
2. Belfast West   5. North Down
3. Belfast South   6. Strangford